# WIGAN

## *A Historical*
## *Souvenir*

# WIGAN

## *A Historical Souvenir*

### BOB BLAKEMAN

SUTTON PUBLISHING LIMITED

First published in the United Kingdom in 1996
Sutton Publishing Limited
Phoenix Mill · Thrupp · Stroud · Gloucestershire · GL5 2BU

British Library Cataloguing in Publication Data
A catalogue record for this book is available from the British Library.

ISBN 0–7509–1475–0

Bob Blakeman hereby asserts his moral right to be identified as the author of this work.

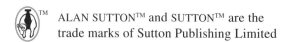

ALAN SUTTON™ and SUTTON™ are the
trade marks of Sutton Publishing Limited

Typeset in 10/12 Times.
Typesetting and origination by
Sutton Publishing Limited.
Printed in Great Britain
WBC, Bridgend, Mid-Glamorgan.

# FOREWORD

By His Worship The Mayor Councillor Bernard Coyle OBE, JP, DL.

Wigan has every reason to feel proud of its past. After all, it is one of the four oldest boroughs in Lancashire.

The first royal charter was granted as long ago as 1246, making the year of its 750th anniversary, 1996, a very special one. I am deeply honoured that this coincides with what is also a very special year for me.

I know that a very full programme of events has been planned by way of celebration, but this book will remain as a lasting souvenir and legacy of 1996, as well as filling a significant gap in the published documentation of the history of the borough.

This 'Historical Souvenir' has been produced to the very high standards which we have come to expect from all Wigan Heritage Service publications. I warmly commend the author on producing, not a conventional history, but rather a collection of historical topics into which the reader can delve as and when he pleases. I particularly like the 'Do You Know?' panels – a novel way of promoting discussion and debate wherever the book is read.

This is a book which all Wiganers, young and old, near and far, will most certainly relish. I warmly commend it to you as a thoroughly fascinating, enjoyable and informative souvenir of Wigan's history, of which we can all feel justly proud.

# ACKNOWLEDGEMENTS

'No man is an island' is an adage that becomes obvious when one writes a book such as this, which covers so many topics. One has to consult the specialists.

So I have taken advice from Len Marsden and Derek Horrocks of the Wigan Family History Society; Tony Meadows of the Wigan Society of Fantasy Films; Wigan Heritage Services Social History Officer Dawn Wadsworth; Industrial History Officer Mike Haddon (who also compiled the sections on Walker Brothers and the Wigan Rugby Club); Leigh Local History Officer Tony Ashcroft (who wrote the section on the Entertainers) and Archivist Nicholas Webb (who helped with the text of the sections on local government and law and order).

Senior Technician Len Hudson worked on the photographs, and graphic artist Max Vitali made my sketch-maps presentable.

Heritage Assistants Hilary Fairclough, Barbara Miller and Stephanie Tsang did the typing and initiated some interesting discussions on points of grammar.

All of the above, and others, made suggestions as to what the book should contain, and thanks are due to them all.

Finally, special thanks are due to the people of Wigan and elsewhere who have deposited old photographs and documents with Wigan Heritage Service. Without them this book would not have been possible.

# CONTENTS

| | |
|---|---|
| Introduction | 9 |
| Roman Wigan | 10 |
| The Barony of Makerfield | 12 |
| Moated Sites | 14 |
| The Mab's Cross Legend | 16 |
| The Medieval Church | 18 |
| Crosses and Chantries | 20 |
| Lords of all they Surveyed | 22 |
| A Country House and Estate | 24 |
| The Decline of the Country House | 26 |
| The Rectors of Wigan | 28 |
| The Church Expands | 30 |
| The Roman Catholics | 32 |
| Dissenting Protestants | 34 |
| The Civil War | 36 |
| Jacobite Plots and Rebellions | 38 |
| The River Douglas | 40 |
| Canals and Coal | 42 |
| The Canals Revived | 44 |
| Coalmining Families | 46 |
| The Pit-brow Lassies | 48 |
| Who Else was at the Pit? | 50 |
| From Coal-face to Fireplace | 52 |
| Accidents and Disasters | 56 |
| Coalmining History Quiz | 58 |
| On the Scrap-heap | 60 |
| Industrial Unrest | 62 |
| Cotton Manufacture | 66 |
| The Mill Girls | 68 |
| Iron and Steel | 70 |
| Walker Bros, Engineers | 72 |
| Roads | 74 |
| Road Transport | 78 |
| The Age of the Tram | 80 |

The Body Builders 82

The Railways 84

Agriculture and Food 86

Hygiene and Public Health 90

House and Home 96

Markets and Shops 102

Local Government 108

The Grammar Schools 114

Wigan Girls' High School 116

The Conservatives 118

The Liberal and Labour Parties 120

Births, Marriages and Deaths 122

Recording Burials 124

Disposal of the Dead 126

The Volunteers 128

The First World War 130

The Second World War 132

Law and Order 134

Pubs and Brewing 136

Do You Remember These Pubs? 138

Local Breweries 140

The Pleasures of the Chase 142

Assorted Sports 144

The Silver Screen 146

The Entertainers 148

Wigan Rugby Club 150

The Power of the Pen 154

The Way It Might Have Been 156

A Weather Note 157

Answers to Questions 158

Sources 159

# INTRODUCTION

It seems to have become something of a tradition for writers, when writing about Wigan, to begin their piece by referring to the town as a 'music-hall joke'. Far be it for Wigan Heritage Services to break with tradition, so we will begin in the same way: by explaining the origin of the 'joke'.

It all began with Wigan Pier, of course. According to the *Oxford English Dictionary*, one of the original meanings of the word 'pier' is 'a projecting landing stage or jetty, on the bank of a river or lake'. In modern times it can also mean 'a pleasure promenade and place of resort' supported on columns over water. A confusion of these two meanings is the basis of the Wigan Pier joke.

During the late eighteenth century canals were cut through the Wigan district to facilitate the transportation of coal from the local collieries. The coal was carried to the canals in wagons which ran on iron rails. The loading points at which the coal was tipped from the wagons into waiting barges were quite correctly called 'piers'. These piers were usually known by the name of the owner of the collieries they served. The nearest to Wigan town centre, situated in an area of warehouses and cotton mills, was Bankes' Pier, which eventually became known as Wigan Pier.

Tradition has it that the Wigan Pier joke began with George Formby snr, a music-hall comedian, and father of the more famous George Formby of film fame, at a time when every seaside resort of note was advertising the attractions of its pier. It was based on the incongruity of an industrial town, miles from the sea, having (as people imagined) a pleasure pier.

By extension, Wigan itself became a joke – a dirty town inhabited by bumpkins – the epitome of provincialism. A comedian had only to get on a stage and shout 'Wigan!' to raise a laugh. In vain the inhabitants tried to publicize their town's venerable history: founded by the Romans; granted a borough charter by King Henry III in 1246, and the Royalist headquarters in Lancashire during the Civil War; but the disparaging image stuck. The Wigan joke was at its height at the time Orwell wrote *The Road to Wigan Pier*: the title was intended to be catchy.

The tipping mechanism on Wigan Pier was dismantled in 1929; only the small elevated brick platform on which it stood remained.

The area around the pier went into decline, and by the late 1970s most of the warehouses were derelict. But in the mid-1980s the area was redeveloped by Wigan Metropolitan Borough Council as a heritage centre with a museum, shop, concert hall, boat trips, a working steam engine, and other attractions. Nowadays thousands of tourists visit Wigan every year, whereas in the 1930s few would have thought of coming here for pleasure. The joke is well and truly dead. . . .

The demolition of Wigan Pier, 1929.

# ROMAN WIGAN

*Coccium*, a settlement mentioned in the Antonine Itinerary of the second century AD as being 17 Roman miles from Manchester, has long been believed to have been on the site of Wigan, but, until recently, evidence of a Roman settlement here had not been conclusive.

The discovery of possibly Roman artifacts in the area goes back a long time. 'Heathen idols' were found under the parish church in 1551, and an altar built into the wall of the church tower may be Roman. A headless statue of Cautopates was unearthed at Appley Bridge in 1932, suggesting the existence in the area of a temple to Mithras, a god who was particularly popular among Roman legionaries. Finds of coins included a hoard of over 200 found in Standish in 1690, and 137 silver ones found near the Boar's Head Inn in 1926. Smaller finds included various bronze coins found in the Market Place in 1837, and a silver coin found at Marylebone in 1930. A rare gold coin of the emperor Vitellius (who reigned for only a few months in AD69) was found in the Mesnes in 1850.

In the early nineteenth century an amateur historian, the Revd E. Sibson of Ashton, was able to trace three Roman roads converging on Wigan. The discovery of a number of cremation urns during the construction of the gas-works in 1822, also suggested the existence of a settlement of some kind. Proof of the existence of a settlement finally came in 1982, when the Greater Manchester Archaeological Unit conducted a series of excavations in the Wiend. The remains of several Roman buildings were found, the earliest dating from the late first century AD. The earlier buildings were flimsy but large, wooden structures of a common warehouse type. Remains of a later period gave evidence of metal working. Unfortunately, no material later than the second century AD was recovered from the site, so it is not possible to state whether occupation continued after that date.

The location was chosen because it was an easily defensible hilltop site, with the River Douglas on two sides. (The sides of the hill sloped away more steeply than they

The probable Roman pagan altar embedded in Wigan parish church tower. It has been defaced with the words '1604 Let Gods worship be.'

do today.) It was also at a point midway between the crossings of the Mersey at Wilderspool and the Ribble at Walton-le-Dale. Similar Roman settlements at these places have yielded material later than the second century AD, so we may yet hope for evidence of a continuing occupation of Roman Wigan.

## *Tracing a Roman Road in 1831*

Much of what we know of the Roman roads in the Wigan area, we owe to the Revd E. Sibson, Vicar of Ashton-in-Makerfield in the early years of the nineteenth century, who traced and described them in detail. Many of the remains that were in evidence in his day have since been destroyed. This is his description of how he found the road over Amerswood Common:

'After many fruitless searches and enquiries, this road was distinctly pointed out, in 1881, by old Thomas Bushell, of Moss House. He said that he and his father before him had been Common-lookers for Mr Walmsley, of Westwood, and that both of them had frequently cut turf on the line of this old road, which runs directly over Amerswood Common, towards Wigan. He said that within his own recollection it had been much more visible than it is at present, and that much of the ridge and gravel of the road had been cut away. The line of the Roman road is, however, very visible over Amerswood Common. In many places it is fourteen yards in breadth, the ridge of the road is broad and round, the grass on the line of it is of a paler green, and wherever it is cut into, the bright gravel of it is found in abundance. At the north end of the Common, near Common Nook, the high ridge of the road and its thick coat of gravel are very prominent.'

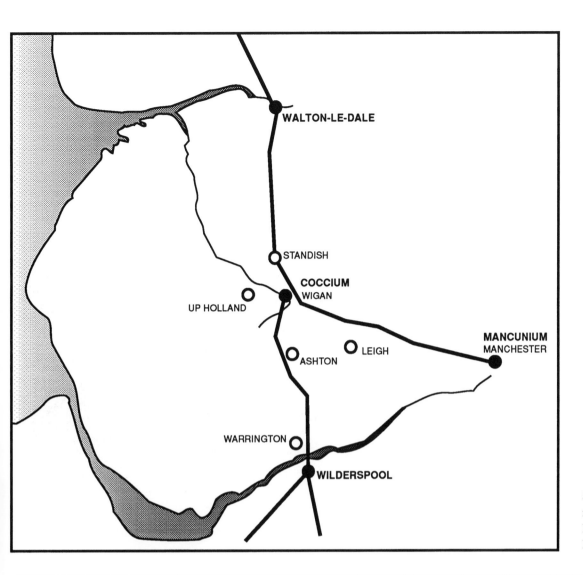

Selected Roman roads between the Ribble and the Mersey.

Two of a hoard of fifty Roman coins discovered near the Boar's Head Inn in 1926. They were found about 10 inches below the surface by a labourer digging a trench, who distributed them amongst his workmates. One of them came to the notice of the Borough Librarian, A.J. Hawkes FSA, who was able to recover them all.

# THE BARONY OF MAKERFIELD

It has been suggested, on place-name evidence, that Makerfield was a British lordship before this part of the country was conquered by the Anglo-Saxons. It was held by the king before the Norman Conquest.

According to a petition presented in Parliament in 1278 by Robert Banastre, Lord of Makerfield, his great-grandfather came to England with William the Conqueror, and acquired, among other lands, the manor of Prestatyn, from which he was driven by the Welsh. As compensation for his loss, he was given a grant from the crown of certain lands within Makerfield, including the demesne lands of Newton and the rectory manor of Wigan, with the advowson of the church there. He was probably merely the farmer or bailiff rather than the lord, because soon after 1204 his descendant Warin Banastre paid 400 marks for the land of Makerfield.

When, some time later, the male line came to an end, the heiress, Alice Banastre married John de Langton (in Leicestershire) after he had paid 250 marks to the Earl of Lancaster for the right to determine whom she should marry. The Barony of Makerfield, with its capital manor at Newton, remained in this family until 1604, when it passed to Richard Fleetwood. In 1660 Thomas Fleetwood sold it to Richard Legh of Lyme, with whose descendants it remains.

In about 1330 the lordship of Hindley was granted to Robert, the younger son of the then Baron Makerfield. This cadet branch of the Langtons continued to be lords of Hindley until 1733, when their seat, Low Hall near Platt Bridge, was sold, together with the manor of Hindley, to the Duke of Bridgewater.

The arms of Thomas Langton, Baron of Newton or Makerfield as recorded in the Herald's visitation of 1533.

Low Hall, seat of the Langtons, lords of Hindley, *c.* 1870.

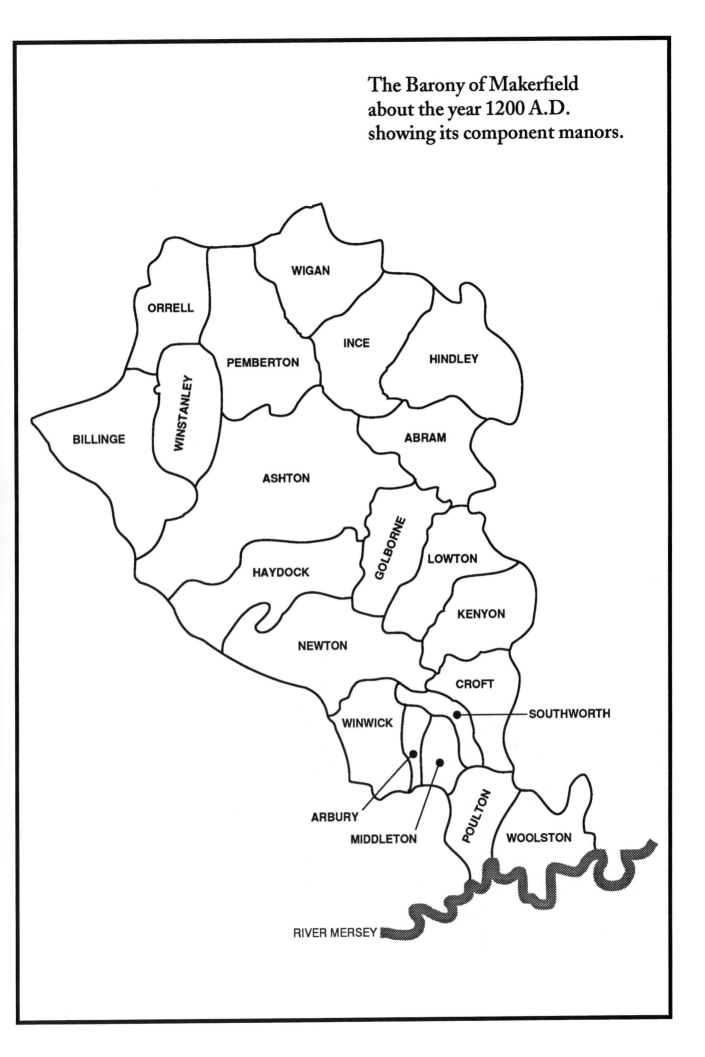

The Barony of Makerfield
about the year 1200 A.D.
showing its component manors.

# MOATED SITES

There are about seventy moated sites in what is now Greater Manchester, and most of them are concentrated around Wigan and Leigh. This is because the topographical and geological conditions were suitable: it is a low-lying area with impermeable subsoil.

The earliest reference to a moated site in the locality is in a grant of 1300, which mentions Peel Hall, Higher Ince. Virtually all the moats in the district were made during the fourteenth century. This was a period of general lawlessness and family feuding, and moats were meant to provide some security against theft and violence by small groups of men.

In other parts of England one commonly finds one moat in each parish, usually situated near a nuclear village. This is not the pattern in Lancashire, however, where even the townships (and there would be several townships in a parish) often have more than one moated site. Ince, for example, has Peel Hall, the Hall of Ince and New Hall. Abram has Abram Hall, Bamfurlong Hall, Bickershaw Hall, and the Bolton Houses site. In the former case, moats protected the manor houses of the lords. The pattern in Lancashire, however, suggests a network of small estates, and is connected with the colonization of wasteland by freemen as the population of a previously under-populated area grew rapidly.

Arley Hall, Blackrod, now the home of Wigan Golf Club.

Gidlow Hall, Aspull. A farmhouse of 1840 has been built within a fourteenth-century moated site.

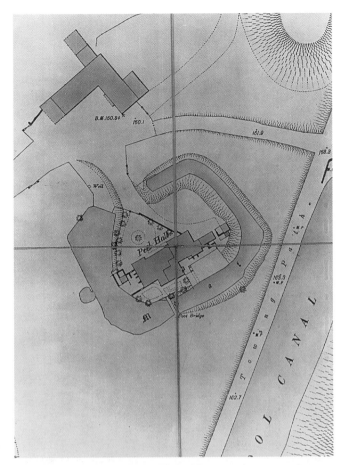

The moated Peel Hall site, Higher Ince, as it appeared on an Ordnance Survey map of 1892.

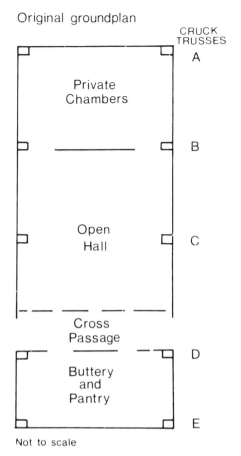

Original groundplan

A plan of Peel Hall as it was in the late thirteenth century. At Norley Hall extra rooms had been added to the basic plan by 1466 (see below). (Greater Manchester Archaeological Unit)

## Norley Hall in 1466

Peter Legh, knight, has one manor within the parish of Wigan and in the hundred called West Derby in the county of Lancaster, formerly the inheritance of the lord Adam of Norley, knight, to wit, one fair hall with one high chamber across the hall above the fireplace, with a chamber called the bedroom, and another chamber below the aforesaid high chamber, and convenient to the said high chamber, and another chamber below the fire-place; with a foodstore or wine-cellar, a pantry, a kitchen, and a great cow-shed for twenty oxen and cows, with a barn, a bakehouse, and a herb-garden with an alder grove; with all the members, messuages, and demesne lands to the said Manor of Norley appearing to or belonging; and the great croft where the said manor house stands, with divers small gardens annexed to the aforesaid Manor, and a small appleyard, which with the said croft contains more than two acres of uncultivated land with divers trees growing therein.

*Legh Terrier* (1466)

# THE MAB'S CROSS LEGEND

The legend of Mab's Cross has come down to us from the fourteenth century. There are two early written accounts which vary slightly. The earliest was written by Sir William Norris of Speke in 1564; the other appears on an ornamental family tree of the Bradshaigh Family drawn up by Randle Holme of Chester in 1647. The following is the Bradshaigh Roll version.

Sir William Bradshaigh of Westleigh married Mabel le Norris, heiress of Haigh. Soon afterwards he left to fight in the crusades. For ten years Lady Mabel had no word from him, and, assuming that he was dead, she married a Welsh knight. But later Sir William returned disguised as a pilgrim. When Lady Mabel saw him, she was, of course, reminded of her husband, and began to weep. The Welsh knight asked why she wept, and when she told him, he struck her. Sir William held his peace; but that night he revealed himself to his faithful retainers. The Welsh knight fled, but Sir William pursued him, and killed him at Newton-le-Willows. Lady Mabel, as a penance for her bigamy, walked barefoot and barelegged once a week from Haigh to the cross which now bears her name.

The Revd Thomas C. Porteus, who discovered the truth behind the Mab's Cross legend.

## *Sir William Bradshaigh and the Banastre Revolt*

In the Middle Ages the kings of England did not have the same degree of power as the later Tudor monarchs. They sometimes faced opposition from powerful barons. The reign of Edward II was one of those periods when friction between the monarch and the barons came to a head. The leader of the baronial opposition was Thomas, Earl of Lancaster, a quarrelsome individual with a knack of making enemies and an inability to inspire loyalty in those who shared his aims.

In the Lancaster fee, the Earl rewarded his favourites with positions of wealth and power, often infringing upon or overriding the heriditary rights of others. The outcome was a revolt by those knights and officials who felt that their power was under threat. Their leader was Sir Adam Banastre, and Sir William Bradshaigh was one of those knights who sided with him.

On 8 October 1315 the disaffected knights met at Wingates near Westhoughton, and, after swearing an oath of allegiance to each other, launched a campaign of violence, theft, and intimidation against the Earl of Lancaster's supporters, the chief among whom was Sir Robert de Holland of Upholland. The court records of the time, written on sheets of parchment and known as the Coram Rege Roll No. 254, paint a vivid picture of their activities. Passages such as the following, which mentions Sir William Bradshaigh, occur several times:

'The jurors of divers wapentakes present that William de Bradeshaghe is a common evil doer, leading a great company of armed men with him in market places and elsewhere in the country (to the terror of the people); and that he beat and wounded Alan de Roucestre at Pemberton, and likewise beat and wounded Henry Gilibrond at Wigan; and he is a common disturber of the king's peace. And they likewise present that the same William entered the enclosure of Thurston de Norley at Norley and hunted beasts in the same close, taking to wit, nine bucks and does belonging to that Thurston and carrying them off against that Thurston's will. . . .'

The rebels ranged across South Lancashire and even into Cheshire (where they captured Halton castle by burning down the gates). Eventually the Deputy Sheriff of Lancashire, Sir Edmund de Nevill, gathered a force of several hundred Lancaster partisans north of the Ribble. The two forces clashed at Deepdale, Preston, and the rebels were routed. Many other Lancaster supporters joined Nevill, and with a force of about two thousand men he moved southwards, searching for fugitive rebels and killing them.

Sir William Bradshaigh escaped, however. Where he had gone, no-one knew; and as the years passed it was assumed that he was dead. (A lawsuit over the manor of Anderton dated 1319 states twice that he was dead.)

Meanwhile the quarrel between the king and the barons continued, and on 16 March 1322 the king defeated Lancaster at the battle of Boroughbridge. The Earl was taken to Pontefract Castle and beheaded.

The political situation in Lancashire had been transformed. Wherever he was, Sir William Bradshaigh heard of the events and returned to claim his estates. We can imagine the joy of Lady Mabel on seeing once again the husband she believed was dead. But they did not settle down in peace and security, for the old feuds continued until the king moved into Lancashire to restore order. Sir William was arrested and held prisoner until 1324 when he was released on a surety of £200. But time was running out for him, and on 16 August 1333 while at Newton-le-Willows he was involved in a fight with members of the Radcliffe family, and was killed. (An attack on the Radcliffes had been the first act in the Banastre Rebellion eighteen years before.)

Before she died Lady Mabel founded two chantries, one at Blackrod and one at Wigan parish church. At her death her body was placed next to that of her husband, in a tomb in Wigan parish church. Carved on the side was the figure of a woman kneeling before a wayside cross.

The story of these events, passed on from generation to generation, and altered in the telling, became the Mab's Cross Legend we know today.

The tomb of Sir William and Lady Mabel Bradshaigh in Wigan parish church, *c*. 1950.

Mab's Cross, in its original position, on the other side of the road from its present situation.

# THE MEDIEVAL CHURCH

Originally the Christian Church in this country was organized on the minster system. A minster was a church and outbuildings surrounded by a palisade or wall and inhabited by a priest and ecclesiastical or secular servants, the priest acting as missionary to the (undefined) surrounding territory. During the ninth and tenth centuries the clergy became attached to proprietorial churches founded by Saxon lords, the boundaries of their manors becoming the boundaries of the parish. Local parishes such as Wigan, Standish, Leigh and Winwick contain several townships, which is considered to be evidence that these parishes were established during this period, although the churches of Wigan and Winwick were probably founded at an earlier date.

In the first quarter of the tenth century the land between the Ribble and the Mersey was annexed to the kingdom of Mercia, and its churches transferred from the then diocese of York to that of Lichfield. St Oswald's, Winwick, is mentioned in the Domesday Book, and Wigan church may have been the 'church of the manor of Newton' mentioned there.

As the churches were founded by lay lords, they had the right to appoint the rectors. The advowson of Wigan church belonged, in the Middle Ages, to the lords of Makerfield. The first known Rector of Wigan, was Ranulf, Treasurer of Salisbury, who was mentioned in 1199. Standish's first known rector was Alexander de Standish, active in 1206.

This part of the country was so sparsely populated and under-developed that not a single monastery had been founded here before the Norman Conquest. But the Conquest ushered in a monastic revival, and many Norman lords made donations of their advowsons to monasteries, who presented the rectors and received from them fixed pensions. However, this failed to completely rid the district of an abuse to which it was particularly subject because of the great size of the parishes and the rectorial manors attached to some of them,

that is the existence of half-secular hereditary parsons. A case in point was that of Leigh, whose first known rector, John, was a married man and was probably not in holy orders. His son Richard, thanks to the more rigid enforcement of the decrees of the first Lateran Council against the occupation of benefices by laymen, was compelled to present a priest to his church in Leigh.

By the end of the twelfth century monasteries were beginning to appropriate the whole property and income of certain benefices, and to appoint paid vicars to see to the 'cure of souls'. Eventually, however, the bishops established their right to the exclusive obedience of the vicars, and the need for an endowment for their support, usually consisting of a portion of land, together with the small tithes. On the other hand, bishops sometimes allowed the rectors to delegate their duties to a vicar at a small fraction of their income. Appropriation by a monastery might be considered beneficial when compared with the way some lay patrons treated their benefices. Advowsons were often used by lay lords as a means of providing a livelihood for their younger sons, whether they were suitable candidates for holy orders or not. Also papal dispensations for pluralities and non-residence were granted to those who had influence; and the crown used its patronage to pay its servants and reward its favourites. A particularly bad example of this was John Mansell, minister of Henry III, who held over 300 benefices, one of which was that of Wigan.

By the fourteenth century Lancashire was well provided with churches and monasteries, and very few others were built in that century. An exception was the Benedictine Priory of Upholland, founded by Sir Robert de Holland in 1319. By this time the lay population had diverted its religious feeling into other channels.

> *DO YOU KNOW?*
> Strictly speaking, Standish parish church is not in Standish. Why not? (Answer on page 158)

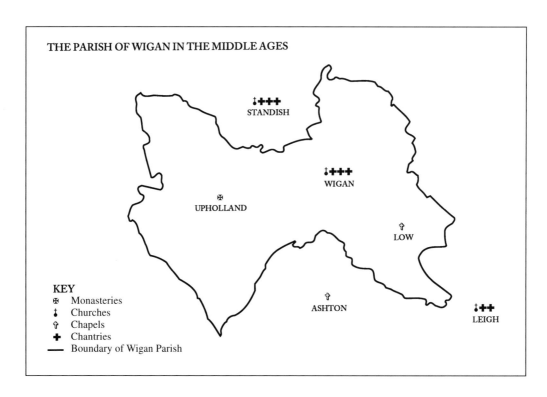

THE PARISH OF WIGAN IN THE MIDDLE AGES

STANDISH

WIGAN

UPHOLLAND

LOW

ASHTON

LEIGH

KEY
✠ Monasteries
⸸ Churches
⳨ Chapels
✚ Chantries
— Boundary of Wigan Parish

Wigan parish church before the rebuilding of 1845–50. The new building was different from the old one only to a small degree; for example, there was no west door, and the tower was raised.

Leigh parish church before the rebuilding of 1873. The present church is taller than the previous one.

Standish parish church. Most of the church dates from a rebuilding of 1562–9, but the tower dates from 1867.

# CROSSES AND CHANTRIES

In the Middle Ages it was common for lay persons to make grants of portions of their land to monastic houses. Sometimes this was in return for the monastery guaranteeing to care for them in their old age. It was a practice among the monks to mark the boundaries of their lands with stone crosses. These were usually broken during the Reformation, but some of their pedestals have survived into the twentieth century. Several can be seen in Standish. Sometimes only the name has survived (for example, Stubshaw Cross and Stone Cross Lane in Golborne); sometimes even the name has fallen out of use in recent times (for example, Culshaw Cross, Lower Ince, and Four-footed Cross, Bryn).

By the beginning of the fourteenth century the religious zeal of the population was turning to the foundation of chantries. This involved providing for a chaplain to sing mass for the souls of those persons specified by the founder, at an altar, usually in a parish church. In this way relief was offered to those souls suffering in purgatory. Sometimes a new chapel was built on to an existing church building, and the founder and his descendants were interred there. Two chantries were established by Lady Mabel Bradshaigh of Mab's Cross fame: one in Wigan parish church and one at Blackrod. Chantries were suppressed in 1547, but the chapels remained the property of the founder's family.

Another expression of medieval religious feeling was the holy wells which were supposed to have curative powers. There is a reference to a 'Holy Well Carr' (i.e. a piece of boggy land) in Wigan near the River Douglas, which probably later became the site of Wigan Spa. On the boundary of Standish and Coppull was Hic Bibi Well, which may have been a holy well, but whose waters have recently run dry. A famous holy well was that known as St Oswald's Well, situated at Hermitage Green in Winwick.

Pedestal of a cross at Standish.

Stump of a medieval cross at St Paul's C. of E. School, Goose Green.

## A Grant of Land to Cockersand Abbey

The following grant of land in Langtree, illustrates how crosses were a common sight in the landscape.

'Grant in frankalmoign from Richard, son of Siward de Langtree (to the canons of Cockersand), of a portion of his land in Langtree within these bounds: from Hare-stane, which is between Langtree and Worthington, following that boundary between the said towns to the great brook which comes down from Langtree, going up that brook unto Belford, and so going up a certain shady place between Little-croft and Wet-butts, through ground which has been ditched and marked out by crosses, unto the cross on the western side of that land, to wit, on the highest point, and so going round that land on the north side as the ground lies where crosses have been placed and ditches made, unto the cross in Green-leach, to wit, on the boundary between Langtree and Worthington, and so following that boundary to Hare-stane again; with common of pasture and other easements, and acquittance of pannage of the pigs of those men dwelling upon that land (who should also be) toll-free.'

(Cockersand Chartulary)

Crosses were not always made of stone. A grant of land in Shevington mentions the 'Dodith oak, marked with the cross'.

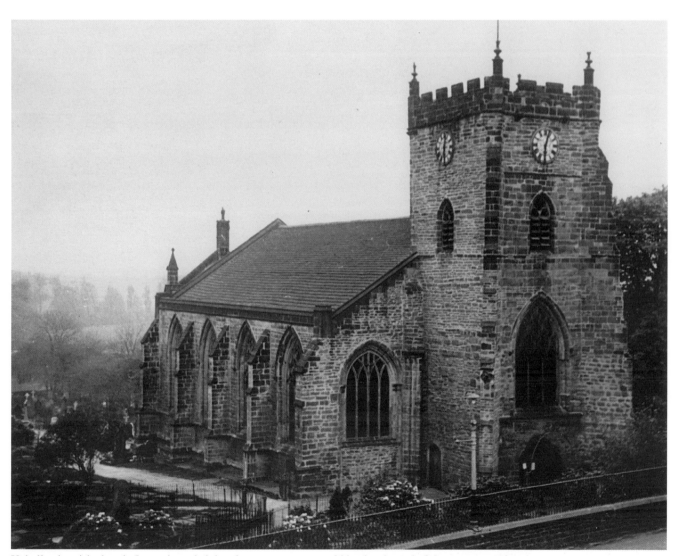

Upholland parish church. It was intended that the present nave would be the chancel of the monastery church.

## The Bradshaigh Family of Haigh Hall

This fine picture by Edward Haytley, painted in 1746, shows Sir Roger Bradshaigh, 4th baronet, and his wife Dorothy, daughter and co-heir of William Bellingham of Levens Hall, Cumbria.

In the background is the earlier Haigh Hall, which was demolished in about 1830. On the crest of a hill to the right is a Gothic folly. Terraces lead down to a lawn and a pond on which there is a boat with rowers. There is an avenue of trees on the left. Sir Roger and Lady Dorothy are shown with objects which make known their interests. On the table next to Sir Roger is a telescope to indicate his scientific pursuits. Lady Dorothy is holding a book. She was a highly intelligent woman who numbered among her friends the writer Samuel Richardson, whose work *Pamela* was the first novel written in English. Richardson visited the Bradshaighs' house in New Bond Street, London, where the painting was hung. He was so impressed with it that he asked Lady Bradshaigh if she would allow him to commission a copy. The copy was made by Joseph Highmore. There are some variations from the original. Sir Roger is shown with his right arm held against his chest, and there is a small deer standing beside Lady Dorothy. We know that the deer's name was Fanny. Presumably Lady Dorothy had a pet parrot as well, as a parrot appears perched on a chair in both versions of the painting. The chairs are in the newly introduced Windsor style. Richardson hung the painting he had commissioned in his house. It appears in the background of a painting of him by Highmore.

The original painting was painted in the year that Sir Roger's father died. Perhaps it was commissioned to commemorate his coming into his inheritance.

Unlike his father, grandfather and great-grandfather, the fourth baronet took no part in either local or national politics. Sir Roger and Lady Dorothy had no children, and their estates passed to Sir Roger's sister's granddaughter, Elizabeth Dalrymple, who married Alexander, 6th Earl of Balcarres, in 1780.

## The Molyneux Family of Hawkley Hall

Painted at Hawkley Hall, Pemberton, by Arthur Devis, the picture above shows Richard Molyneux (died 1762) with his wife Jane, and his sons Richard, Bryan and William. The Molyneux family had owned and occupied Hawkley since the middle of the fourteenth century when Roger Molyneux, second son of Alan Molyneux of Rainhill, married the daughter and sole heiress of Gilbert Ince of Hawkley. When the last of the direct male line died in 1805 he was succeeded by a distant relation, Revd William Hockenhull, who assumed the name and arms of Molyneux. His son, Revd Bryan William Molyneux, sold the estate to Meyrick Bankes of Winstanley Hall in 1840, who intended to exploit the coal seams there. Coal had been worked there on a small scale for at least a century before. In 1776 the coal mines were only worth £100, compared with the timber on the plantations, which was worth £1,000.

# A COUNTRY HOUSE AND ESTATE

During the sixteenth century the gentry began to bring the park (formerly an enclosure for hunting) and the mansion together, the park palisade or wall creating a private environment separate from the rest of the estate, which was devoted to agriculture and industry, and let to tenants. Large ornamental gates were set within the wall to allow for entry and exit. At the gates lodges were built, occupied by keepers to ensure that unauthorized persons did not enter. At the outer edge of the park would be a farm, usually known as Home Farm, which provided the inhabitants with fresh food in the days before canning and freezing. There may also have been extensive workshops where essential maintenance work was carried out, a house for the estate steward, and an estate office which was the administrative centre. The area within the park would be landscaped to improve the view, perhaps with artificial lakes and ruins. Close to the mansion would be the stable block so that horses and carriages could be brought quickly to the inhabitants. Occasionally one might have found a private church or chapel next to the house.

The stable block at Haigh Hall. This was built about twenty years after the hall itself.

Home Farm on the Haigh Hall estate.

Basin Lane (or Hall Lane) Lodge, on the Haigh Estate. It was possible for the gate-keeper to open the gates without leaving the building, simply by turning a brass wheel inside the lodge.

Workshops at Haigh Hall.

Haigh Estate Office, New Road.

# THE DECLINE OF THE COUNTRY HOUSE

A large-scale destruction of country houses took place in the Wigan area from the middle of the nineteenth through to the end of the twentieth century. Two factors were mainly responsible; the first being the multiplicity of small estates, each with its own small 'capital messuage', which meant that landowners with more than one estate would choose to live on a larger one. The second factor was the growth of industry, which meant again that landlords would prefer to live outside the area unless actively involved in local industry (as were the Earls of Crawford, for example). Once a landowner had decided not to live in a house, a certain pattern of decline could be observed. First, it would be let to a local industrialist (for example, Standish Hall was let to a cotton manufacturer in 1825); then, moving down the social scale, to a professional (Ince Hall was let to the manager of Rose Bridge Colliery); or it might become a farmhouse (as did Hawkley Hall). The next stage would be for it to be divided into several dwellings (for example, the Hall of Ince); and as a final degradation used for industrial purposes (Low Hall was used for storing carts). Natural disasters have also taken their toll. Bispham Hall was gutted by fire in 1978; Urmston-in-the-Meadows disappeared under Pennington Flash as the land sank.

Preserving local halls was a problem because the wealthy no longer wanted to live in them. Most of Standish Hall was demolished when it failed to reach the reserve price at auction in 1921. Only corporate bodies have been able to save the halls by altering their function. Wigan Golf Club bought Arley Hall, Wigan Corporation bought Haigh Hall, and Birchley Hall was converted to medical use.

The demolition of Pennington Hall, Leigh, after the discovery of extensive dry rot there in 1963.

---

*DO YOU KNOW?*
Where is The Hall, Wigan? (Answer on page 158)

---

Low Hall as it was shortly before demolition, when it was used for storing carts. Compare with the illustration on page 12.

Bispham Hall, one of the finest Elizabethan buildings in Lancashire, was gutted by fire in 1978.

The fourteenth-century moated site of Urmston-in-the-Meadows disappeared under Pennington Flash.

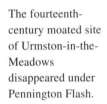

At the time of writing Winstanley Hall had been on the market for some time. What fate awaits this fine house?

# THE RECTORS OF WIGAN

During the Anglo-Saxon period local lords began to build churches on their manors to serve themselves and their tenants. As these churches were originally private foundations the founders' descendants retained the right of advowson; that is, the right to nominate a clergyman to a benefice, subject to the approval of a diocesan bishop. In the Middle Ages the advowson of Wigan parish church was held by the Langtons as Barons of Makerfield. In the early part of the seventeenth century it passed to Richard Fleetwood of Calwich, Staffordshire, who was cousin to Sir Thomas Langton, last of the direct male line. Richard Fleetwood's son sold it to Sir Orlando Bridgeman soon after the Restoration. It remained in the Bridgeman family until recently, when the Earl of Bradford donated it to the Bishop of Liverpool.

Generally, if a church has a rector assigned to it, it is almost certainly an old foundation. In the Middle Ages, when a benefice was annexed by a corporate body such as a monastery, the corporate body nominally became the rector, and appointed a vicar (the word means representative or substitute) to see to the day-to-day running of the parish.

Thomas Linacre, the eminent classical scholar and founder of the College of Physicians, was Rector of Wigan from 1519 to 1524.

Below is a list of some of the Rectors of Wigan. Note how often the names Langton and Bridgeman appear, showing how the patrons used the advowson to provide livings for members of their family.

1334 – John de Langton

1344 – John de Cravene

1349 – John de Winwick

1359 – Richard de Langton

1359 – Robert de Lostock

1361 – Walter de Compeden

1370 – James de Langton

1415 – William de Langton

1432 – James de Langton

1451 – Oliver de Langton

1485 – John de Langton

1504 – Thomas Langton

1741 – Roger Bridgeman

1776 – Guy Fairfax (first cousin of the wife of Henry Bridgeman)

1790 – George Bridgeman

1833 – Henry J. Gunning (nephew to Henry Bridgeman)

1864 – Hon. G.T.O. Bridgeman

Dr John Bridgeman was Rector from 1616 to 1643. His diary or journal is an important source for the early seventeenth-century history of Wigan.

The Bridgeman arms on the rectory gatehouse in Frog Lane.

The Hon. and Revd G.T.O. Bridgeman was Rector of Wigan from 1864 to 1895. He was also an honorary canon of Liverpool Cathedral and Chaplain in Ordinary to Queen Victoria.

# THE CHURCH EXPANDS

By the early nineteenth century private box pews for the middle classes filled the bodies of most parish churches, to the detriment of the labouring people. Often, during services, people would be crowded in the aisles, while pews were empty. This picture shows the box pews at St Aidan's Church, Billinge.

Over the years private pews were abolished. Here is the more flexible and egalitarian seating system introduced into some churches. Such arrangements encouraged more people to attend church services.

In the early nineteenth century the government, concerned that revolutionary ideas might spread among the working classes, voted over a million pounds for church-building. The churches built with this money were known as Commissioners' Churches. They were often cheaply built and austere in style. St John's, Pemberton, and St David's, Haigh (shown here), are examples.

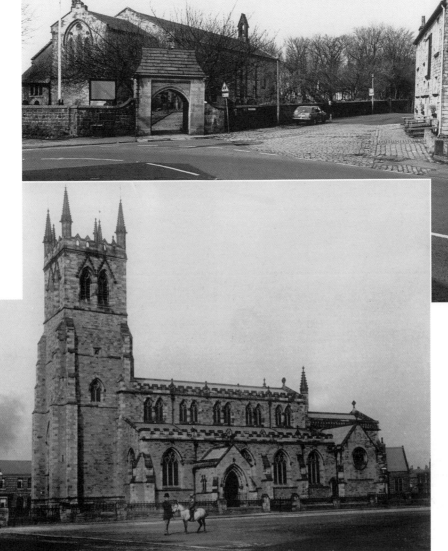

At the other extreme were those churches which were paid for by local industrialists. They were built to impress, and were often too large for the parishes they served. St James', Poolstock, shown here, was built by mill-owner Nathanial Eckersley.

Whenever the Church of England moved into a new district, a school would be built first, and used on Sundays as a church. A church would be built later, when money was available. This is St Barnabas' Mission Church and School, Marsh Green. (A. Bradbury)

# THE ROMAN CATHOLICS

The history of Roman Catholic churches in England may be divided into three broad periods. The first was the period of the strict application of anti-Catholic laws. These began with the Acts of Uniformity of 1552 and 1559, which imposed fines for non-attendance at Church of England services. The laws increased in severity until by 1584 it was high treason for laymen to receive the ministrations of Roman Catholic priests. During this period Catholic activity had to be kept secret. The survival of the Roman Catholic church in England came to depend upon the Roman Catholic gentry, who provided hiding places in their houses for English Catholic missionary priests. Religious services were held in rooms designed for other purposes: there were no Roman Catholic churches.

Gradually the penal laws began to be applied less strictly. The Roman Catholic gentry began to set rooms aside permanently for religious use. The next stage was for purpose-built chapels to be erected in the grounds of the house, or built on to it (as at Standish Hall and Westwood House, Lower Ince). During this period the Catholics were tolerated, but viewed with suspicion. The authorities periodically took note of their number and their names, and they are recorded in various documents (for example, the Returns of Papists). These show that the Catholics were found in groups, each group under the protection of a gentry family.

The third period is that following the Catholic Relief Act of 1791, which enabled Catholics to worship at their own registered churches under registered priests, and many churches were built. Catholicism became an urban religion as a result of the growth of industrial towns and large-scale Irish immigration to them.

The Tudor wing of Wrightington Hall during demolition in 1929. The top arrow shows the priest hole, exit from which was by way of a cupboard. The lower arrow shows one of the three exits; this one leading to the basement.

Standish Hall, showing the Roman Catholic chapel on the right. It was built in 1742–3.

# Returns of Papists 1767

*Ashton Quarter in the Parish of Winwick*

| Names | Occupation | Age | How long resident |
|---|---|---|---|
| Sir Thomas Gerrard | | 42 | 42 years |
| Lady Gerrard | | 42 | 19 |
| Elizabeth | | 16 | 16 |
| Catherine | their children | 10 | 10 |
| Mary | | 6 | 6 |
| Mr Green | a priest | 55 | 12 |
| Mrs Hulme | | 80 | 18 |
| Cook | | 36 | 8 |
| Elizabeth Greenough | | 22 | 4 |
| Ellen Calland | | 25 | 5 |
| Ellen Spencer | | 30 | 3 |
| Ann Keighley | | 32 | 6 |
| Ann Jolley | | 36 | 10 |
| Joseph Lythgoe | servants | 28 | 6 |
| John Boardman | | 30 | 9 |
| Nicholas Grimshaw | | 30 | 3 |
| Henry Blundell | | 40 | 6 |
| Robert Barns | | 40 | 12 |
| Mary Barns | | 32 | 7 |
| Inley Riding | | 30 | 4 |
| Margaret Dagnell | | 28 | 3 |
| James Fletcher | brewer to Sir Thomas | 45 | 17 |
| Ellen his wife | | 30 | 17 |
| James | | 10 | 10 |
| Mary | their children | 8 | 8 |
| James Bankes | gardener to Sir Thomas | 67 | 67 |
| John Hodkinson | Auditor to Sir Thomas Gerrard's coal pits | 40 | 16 |
| Mary his wife | | 40 | 40 |
| Thomas Appleton | Gamekeeper to Sir Thomas Gerrard | 45 | 20 |
| Jane his wife | | 40 | 20 |

There were 382 Roman Catholics listed in Ashton-in-Makerfield, and 796 in the whole of Winwick Parish. By contrast there was one only in the whole parish of Bury.

St Mary's Roman Catholic church, Standishgate, was built in 1818–19, the same year as nearby St John's. St Mary's was served by the secular clergy, and St John's by the Jesuits.

# DISSENTING PROTESTANTS

During the seventeenth century several Protestant groups emerged outside the Church of England. Such were the Baptists, Presbyterians, Congregationalists and Quakers. They had in common an opposition to a church structure consisting of archbishops, bishops and an appointed parish clergy; and a desire to simplify the liturgy. They differed in what they stood for, however, the Baptists advocating adult baptism, the Congregationalists wanting an elected clergy, and the Quakers wanting no clergy at all. (In these they all saw themselves reverting to the values of the early Christian Church.) They were persecuted or restricted until the Toleration Act of 1689 allowed them to build their own chapels.

During the eighteenth century another series of Protestant denominations came into existence as the Methodist movement broke away from the Church of England, and splintered into several different groupings. Methodism was strong among the working-class and was evenly spread throughout the town and country. 'Old Dissent' was strongest amongst the urban middle classes. Neither had the financial resources of the Church of England or the Roman Catholic Church, and many chapels were of the simplest design and constructed of the cheapest materials. In Wigan, increasing prosperity meant that these early chapels were often re-built in a more imposing style (for example St Paul's, Standishgate, Hope Chapel, and Trinity Presbyterian in Chapel Lane).

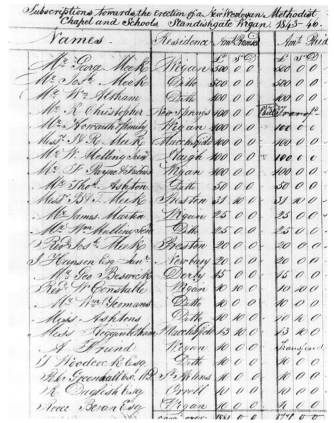

A record of donations paid towards the erection of the Wesleyan Methodist chapel and schools in Standishgate. The large amounts given by business donors enabled the congregation to build a more substantial chapel than most.

A minister at Trinity Presbyterian chapel in Chapel Lane. The academic style of ceremonial robe shows how the Presbyterians stressed learning and understated ritual.

The interior of St Paul's Congregational chapel, Standishgate. The pulpit has pride of place, showing the importance the dissenters placed on preaching.

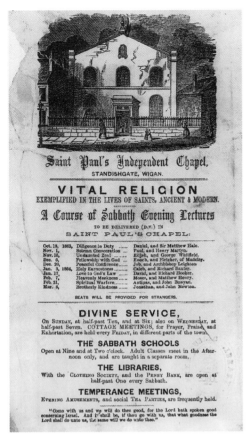

A publicity notice for St Paul's Congregational chapel, showing various expressions of dissent, such as the use of the word 'Sabbath' for 'Sunday' and the cottage and temperance meetings.

A new development in the mid-nineteenth century was the introduction into England of churches of American origin. This is the Church of Christ in Rodney Street.

Revivalist meetings were popular in the nineteenth and early twentieth centuries. This one was at Golborne in 1901.

# THE CIVIL WAR

At the outbreak of the Civil War geographical location and class structure were the main factors determining whether a locality was for the King or for Parliament. Generally speaking the south and east of England was for Parliament, and the north and west for the King. Aristocratic landowners and their tenants and those who did business with them were Royalist; the independent lesser gentry and merchants were for Parliament. Wigan was only a few miles from Lathom House, the seat of the Earl of Derby, and was garrisoned by his troops. The town, strategically situated on the main north–south route, was fought over several times. Oliver Cromwell passed through here once, in 1648, his troops engaged in a running battle with the Duke of Hamilton's Royalists. The Royalist cause in Lancashire sustained its final defeat here on 25 August 1651 at the battle of Wigan Lane.

Artisans and labourers were agitating for political rights in the town before the outbreak of the war. This was the political environment out of which emerged Gerrard Winstanley, spokesman for the Diggers or True Levellers, and author of several important works of radical polemics.

Sir Thomas Tyldesley, the epitome of cavalier gallantry, was killed at the battle of Wigan Lane on 25 August 1651.

After the Restoration Alexander Rigby, Sir Thomas' cornet at Wigan Lane, had this monument erected to his memory.

# A Contemporary Account of the Battle of Wigan Lane

The following letter was written immediately after the event, by the commander of Parliament's forces at the battle of Wigan Lane and sent to the Honourable William Lenthall Esq., Speaker of the Parliament.

Mr Speaker,

My Lord Generall being pleased to command me to stay here to assist the well-affected against the Lord Derby, who was then at Warrington in this County, with some considerable force both from the Isle of Man, and which he had from the Scots army, wherewith he did not only much encourage the Enemies, but also discourage all the well-affected in these Counties of Lancashire and Cheshire, and whereof he thought himselfe wholly Master (as indeede he was), and none in those Counties were able, or durst appear against him; and began to beate Drums, and raise men in all places where he came, and would have been very strong in a short time, not only through the accesse of many Malignants, Papists, and disaffected Persons, but that assistance the Ministers and those who are called Presbyterians afforded, and would more abundantly have appeared, for they are the men who are grown here more bitter and envious against you than others of the old Cavaliers stamp; the power of the Almighty was very much seene in the total overthrow (I hope) of that wicked designe which was laid and hatched not only here, but through the whole North of England, which was getting into the like posture, as you may further understand by those papers I have here sent you; but that God who hath all along appeared with us and for us, hath shewed himself very good, and powerful in the discipating of this Enemy, who was about fourteen to fifteen hundred strong; I had only three companies of Foot, about fifty or sixty Dragoons, and about thirty Horse from Liverpoole, with my own wearied and somewhat scattered Regiment through our tedious March from Scotland, and hard duty we had here.

Yesterday morning, about eleven or twelve a clock in the night, the Enemy marched from Preston, we lying within two or three miles of them, where we expected those supplyes of Forces which came not, some of our intelligence informing us the Enemy were running away towards their army with what they had gotten; we pursued them hither with some confidence, that that intelligence was true, and the rather we believed it because of some discouragement we put upon them the day before; but upon our approach hither we found it otherwise, for they were bending their course towards Manchester, where they had not only very great hopes of surprising my Lord Generall's Regiment of Foot, but also assurance of the assistance of five hundred men in and about that Towne, but, upon the sight of our near approach, they unexpectedly put themselves in a posture of fighting with us, which then we endeavoured to decline, in regard to the very great advantage they had by their many Foote and Hedges, and the danger we apprehended my Lord Generall's Regiment of Foot at Manchester to be in, we were drawing off, thinking to have marched in the left flanke of them thither, to have gained a conjunction with our Friends, who too, had order to march that day to me to Preston; we had thought to have met them on the way, having sent severall messengers to let them know both the Enemies and our motion, but the enemy perceiving us to draw off, quickly advanced upon us with their Horse and Foot, which we perceiving, and that we could not goe off safely enough, we fell to dispute with them, which lasted almost one houre; our horse being not able to doe any service but in Lanes, and they overpowering us so much in Foot, made the businesse very difficult that we hardly knew whose the day would be for so long; but therein was the Salvation of God the more seen, and the greater opportunity we had to destroy them. I desire that he may have the praise and glory of that happy successe he was pleased to give unto his poor creatures. Having given you this narrative in general, which I thought it my duty to doe, this inclosed list will inform you further of the particulars. I desire the Lord would teach us to walke in some way answerable to those manifold and gracious Dispensations he daily gives us experience of, and manifests his love to us, in that, His name may be magnified in all we do in our severall places and stations; this great mercie to us here I hope is the earnest of his further tendernesse to the great concernment of all good people in this Nation, which is the hearty desire of

Yours faithful and most humble Servant to my power,

ROB. LILBURNE.

This Bearer was all the while in the Engagement, and is able to give you further Relation.

I have not lost an Officer in this Engagement, but one Corporal, and not above ten souldiers slaine, but very many wounded.

Present these

To the Right Honourable William Lenthall, Esq., Speaker of the Parliament of the Common Wealth of England. – Haste.

A List of the Prisoners taken at Wigan, August 25th, 1651.

| | |
|---|---|
| Col. Throgmorton | All their Baggage and Sumptures, Armes and Ammunition, the L. Derbies three Cloakes with Stars, his George, Garter, and other Robes. |
| Col. Rich. Leg | |
| Col. John Robbinson | |
| Col. Baynes | ——— |
| Col. Ratcliffe Gerret | Slaine and dead since they were taken. |
| Adjutant General | The L. Witherington |
| Lieut-Col. Creson Rigby | Major-Gen. Sir Tho. Tilsley |
| Lieut-Col. Francis Baynes | Col. Math. Boynton |
| Lieut-Col. Galliard | Major Chester |
| Lieut-Col. Constable | Major Trollop, and divers others of quality, |
| Major Gower | whose names are not yet brought in, besides |
| Four Captains, 2 Lieutenants | 60 private men. |
| One Quarter-master | |
| Twenty Gentlemen and Reformadoes | |
| 400 Private Prisoners | |

# JACOBITE PLOTS AND REBELLIONS

When King James II claimed he had the power to set aside the laws of the realm and attacked the Church of England in the interests of Roman Catholicism, England's protestant ruling élite invited his son-in-law William of Orange to take the throne, and James was forced to flee the country in 1688.

James still had his supporters, however, especially among the Roman Catholics in Lancashire, and for some years afterwards the air was full of rumours of plots to restore the Stuarts. One of the most spectacular events arising from this tense atmosphere was the Lancashire Jacobite plot of 1694, when eight men including Sir William Gerard of Bryn, William Dicconson of Wrightington and Philip Langton of Hindley were tried for treason at Manchester, largely on the strength of information provided by government informers. They were all acquitted, largely on account of the testimony given by John Taffe, a former government informer, who declared that the plot had been invented by himself and his fellow spies. At the next Lancashire Assizes the accused successfully prosecuted for perjury the three chief witnesses against them, who were sentenced to periods of imprisonment. The government was seriously embarrassed, and the following year the law concerning the treason trials was changed.

However, years later, in 1757, a bundle of papers was discovered, hidden in a wall at Standish Hall, which related to these events. But it was not until after the death of the last of the Standishes in 1920 that the papers were examined properly. The government informers were completely vindicated. Here were letters indicating the plotters' intentions; declarations of loyalty to James signed by his supporters in Lancashire; lists of appointments made by James in preparation for the time when he should be restored to the throne; blank commissions sealed and signed by James; accounts of the numbers of government forces; and military instructions. The government of the time had been well and truly duped.

James II never returned to England, however, and following the death of Queen Anne, George, Elector of Hanover, succeeded to the throne. The Jacobites thought that there would be little support for a German king, and in 1715 a Jacobite army raised in Scotland invaded England and marched into Lancashire. By the time they arrived in Preston two government armies were converging upon them; one under General Carpenter was moving down the Ribble valley and another, under General Wills, was moving northwards from Wigan. Wills' force arrived first, and the Jacobites managed to repulse it. But the next day it was joined by General Carpenter's army. Preston was surrounded and the Jacobites heavily outnumbered. After a brief fight they surrendered.

For thirty years little was heard of the Jacobites. But in 1745, when England was engaged in a war in Europe, Charles Edward, the grandson of James II, and generally known nowadays as Bonnie Prince Charlie, landed in the Hebrides. He crossed the border with an army of about six thousand and by 27 November was in Preston. He intended to march south via Wigan and Warrington, but his plan had to be changed because the government had had the bridge at Warrington pulled down to delay his advance. So he marched to Manchester, and then south and east to Derby. By this time his officers felt that they were marching into a trap, and persuaded the Prince to retreat. By 9 December they were back in Manchester, and then moved to Wigan where the Prince lodged in Walmesley House in Bishopgate. Some of the Highland troops were billeted in the old grammar school in Rodney Street. Before them lay the long retreat to Scotland and final defeat at Culloden.

Walmesley House (sometimes called the Manor House) in Bishopgate. Bonnie Prince Charlie lodged here on 10 December 1745.

# By the King,
# A PROCLAMATION,

For Apprehending of *William Standish* of *Standish-Hall* in the County of *Lancaster*, Esquire.

## WILLIAM R.

Hereas His Majesty hath received Information, That William Standish of Standish-Hall in the County of Lancaster, Esquire, hath Conspired, with divers other Disaffected Persons, to Disturb and Destroy the Government, and for that purpose bought up Arms, and Abetted and Adhered to His Majesties Enemies ; For which cause several Warrants have Issued for the Apprehending of the said William Standish, but he hath withdrawn himself from his usual Place of Abode, and is fled from Justice : His Majesty therefore hath thought fit, by and with the Advice of His Privy Council, and upon an Humble Address from the House of Commons for that purpose, to Issue this His Royal Proclamation ; And His Majesty doth hereby Command and Require all His Loving Subjects to Discover, Take and Apprehend the said William Standish wherever he may be found, and to Carry him before the next Justice of Peace, or Chief Magistrate, who is hereby Required to Commit him to the next Gaol, there to remain until he be thence delivered by due Course of Law. And His Majesty doth Require the said Justice, or other Magistrate immediately to give Notice thereof to His Privy Council, or one of the Principal Secretaries of State. And His Majesty doth hereby Publish and Declare, That all Persons who shall Conceal the said William Standish, or be Aiding or Assisting in Concealing him, or furthering his Escape, shall be Proceeded against for such their Offence, with the utmost Severity according to Law. And His Majesty does hereby Promise, That whosoever shall Discover and Apprehend the said William Standish, and Bring him before some Justice of Peace, or Chief Magistrate, shall have and Receive the Reward of Five hundred Pounds for so doing. And We do hereby Authorize and Require Our present Commissioners of Our Treasury, and Our High Treasurer and Commissioners of Our Treasury for the time being, to make Payment of the said Sum accordingly.

Given at Our Court at *Kensington* the Fourteenth Day of *March* 1694. In the Seventh Year of Our Reign.

## God save the King.

*London*, Printed by *Charles Bill*, and the Executrix of *Thomas Newcomb* deceas'd, Printers to the Kings most Excellent Majesty. 1694.

A royal proclamation ordering the arrest of William Standish for plotting with other Jacobites to overthrow the government.

# THE RIVER DOUGLAS

The River Douglas rises in the moors above Rivington, from where it flows in a south-westerly direction until it reaches the hill on which Wigan stands. It skirts the hill to the south and then alters its course to flow in a north-westerly direction and eventually reach the Ribble estuary.

The name Douglas is derived from a Celtic word meaning 'black water'. It acquired its name and its colour from the geological coal measures over which it flows in the Wigan area. In its lower course it used to be known as the Asland.

According to the Welsh historian Nennius, King Arthur fought several battles on the banks of a River Dunglas. This river has never been identified, and the Douglas is one of the candidates.

Looking at the shallow stream that is the Douglas today, it is difficult to realize that it played an important part in the economy of the district. Before the invention of steam power, moving water was the chief means of driving machinery. Along the course of the upper Douglas, every half mile or less a watermill of some kind could be found. These mills performed various functions: they ground corn, ground log wood, and processed woollen cloth. One even worked the cage at a colliery.

A major engineering project in the early eighteenth century was the Douglas Navigation, which made the river navigable from Wigan to the Ribble estuary. The Navigation was a precursor of the nationwide network of canals that was to act as a springboard for the Industrial Revolution.

The River Douglas with Westwood Power Station in the background. In earlier centuries weirs were built across the river to provide a flow of water forceful enough to drive waterwheels.

Floods used to occur frequently on the banks of the Douglas. The locations most liable to flooding were lower Wallgate (Pottery Terrace is shown here) and Scholes Bridge.

# The Floods at Wigan

We noticed, last week, the overflow of the river Douglas, and the drowning of the collieries in that neighbourhood. We are sorry to have to record, that, notwithstanding every attempt made to lower the water, and get at the bodies of the unfortunate men, who were in the mine at the time of the inundation, the waters have again got the upper hand; and there is no chance but that the works must remain stopped for months, and 1200 people thrown out of employment. The coal proprietors, affected by these disasters, met on Wednesday, and resolved on plans for securing the river from causing further damage. On a careful examination of the bed of the river, it was found that the old mines had been worked to within 2 yards from the surface; and, from the action of the waters, nothing but a thin crust was left between it and the hollows, and the water penetrated in several places; all approaches to the mines were bricked up, and a new shaft was to be sunk for the two mines. All was proceeding rapidly up to Saturday last – the sides and bed of the river were well puddled and secured, as it was thought, with piles and planking, when, on Saturday evening, the heavy floods of rain, which poured in torrents all day, penetrated beneath the puddling, washed down the wooden barriers, rushed into the mine through the hollows, poured down the shafts in streams, and continued until Sunday afternoon. The pumps continued working, but the water gained upon them; and, on examination, it was found that the shafts were 130 yards deep in water, and still gaining, and in the evening it reached 150 yards. On Monday morning all hopes were given up – every barrier had been washed away, planks and piles washed into the mines, and great fears were entertained, that the two overflowed fields would sink into the excavations beneath. Many parts of the neighbourhood on which buildings are erected, are known to be undermined to within a few feet of the foundations, and the greatest alarm exists in the district.

'The inundation of the collieries at Wigan will, it is now calculated (says a contemporary), throw nearly a thousand hands out of work for months to come, and a new and fearful interest has been given to the catastrophe in the neighbourhood by an opinion given currency to by some of the more experienced miners of a possibility that the ill-fated work-people in the mine may still be alive. At a meeting in Wigan, on Wednesday night, at which upwards of 500 colliers were present, this opinion was maintained, and is set forth in the following address to the House of Commons, agreed to at that meeting'.

'To the Honourable the House of Commons in Parliament assembled: The humble petition of the undersigned, residing in and near to Wigan, Lancashire, wives, children, relations, and friends of four men and two boys now in the Lower Patricroft, humbly showeth, that on Tuesday or Wednesday last, the water from the River Douglas, in Wigan, broke its banks, and overflowed into the coal mine called Lower Patricroft, and where there were then working John Rutter, the elder, John Rutter, the younger, Mathew Bates, Thomas Roch, John Sherry and Michael Underwood, colliers. That these six persons were not able to get out of the pit, in consequence of the water, and that they are still in the pit, but whether they are dead or alive your petitioners cannot tell. That the rush of water has been so great that the engines of the coalmasters have not been able to keep down the water, and with the present engine power it must be many weeks, and perhaps months, before the water can be got out sufficiently to recover the six unfortunate persons who are now in the pit. Your petitioners humbly implore your honourable House to send down some greater engine power, to raise out the water and to block out the river; for your petitioners think it possible that the before-named six persons may be out of the water, but not able to get to the shaft, and that by great exertions their lives might be saved. And your petitioners will ever pray.' & c.

Two colliers, named Ingham and Bury, who are sufferers by the calamity, were the principal speakers at the meeting, and a series of temperate resolutions were drawn up, in addition to the above petition, and passed, in which the colliers expressed an opinion, that under the unexpected destitution which had overtaken them, they should be justified in applying to the guardians of the poor for relief, without being compelled, as under ordinary circumstances, to pledge their clothes and break up household establishments.

*Mining Journal* (1847)

# CANALS AND COAL

One of the major effects of the Douglas Navigation was the increased extraction of coal which it encouraged in the Wigan coalfield. The chief reason for its construction was to facilitate the transport of coal to the Irish Sea markets. But the largest market for Wigan coal was the port of Liverpool, and the Douglas Navigation did not connect the two towns directly. By 1765, however, the Duke of Bridgewater had constructed a canal from his collieries at Worsley to Manchester, which was so successful that the imagination of the country was fired and many more canal schemes were thought up. One of these was a canal linking Leeds and Liverpool, which finally opened throughout the whole route in 1816. By December 1820 a branch had been constructed from Wigan connecting the Leeds and Liverpool with the Bridgewater Canal at Leigh. In spite of the phenomenal expansion of the railway network during the nineteenth century, the Leeds and Liverpool Canal continued to be a major means of transporting coal until well into the first half of the twentieth century.

A coal tippler at Douglas Bank Colliery.

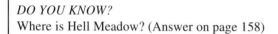

DO YOU KNOW?
Where is Hell Meadow? (Answer on page 158)

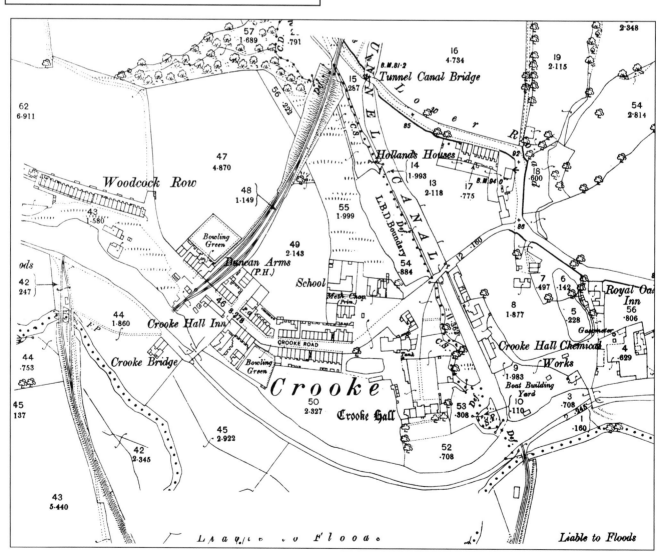

Map showing part of the Tunnel Canal constructed by the Standish Coal Company in 1807. Just to the north of the map were about 600 yds of underground canal ending at the coal face.

Coal barges near Gathurst.

Coal barges at Dean Lock. Before the completion of the Leeds and Liverpool Canal, boats from the partly built canal joined the Douglas Navigation here.

The preserved shortboat *Roland* at Wigan Pier.

# THE CANALS REVIVED

Coal boats delivering coal from Bickershaw Colliery to Westwood Power Station were the last industrial traffic of any importance on the canal. The service ended in 1972, and there was no further use for the boats.

Numerous pleasure boats now cruise the canal. This scene is at Crooke, where there was once a pier for loading coal on to barges.

Derelict stone warehouses at Wigan Pier before renovation.

The Wigan Pier heritage centre complex, now a major tourist attraction, was opened by HM the Queen on 21 March 1986. (L. Hudson)

# COALMINING FAMILIES

In the Middle Ages miners were freemen, and ranked above the feudal peasantry. Manual work in the pits was performed by family groups. Adult males hewed the coal while children and adult females moved it to the surface. Jobs were passed on from one generation to another in the same family.

By the middle of the nineteenth century this family-based system was breaking down. Adult women were only a small proportion of the workforce, but were concentrated in a few coalfields, one of which was the Wigan coalfield. Women in the Wigan coalfield wore a distinctive dress consisting of trousers which came down to the calves or ankles and a short skirt, which was sometimes longer at the back than at the front. This costume ceased to be worn at the end of the nineteenth century.

Perhaps the child workers suffered most from the breakdown of the family system, because it loosened the emotional bond between the hewer and the drawer, who was dependent on the hewer for his pay or provisions. A government enquiry in 1841 uncovered a shocking state of affairs. Apart from disquiet about the over-work, dangerous conditions, ignorance and brutality suffered by women and children, Victorian moral susceptibilities were outraged at the thought of half-naked adults and children crawling about in the dark. An Act of 1842 banned boys under ten years old, and all females from working underground.

A collier poses for the camera with his equipment.

Dirt and coal dust were everywhere at the pit.

# Child Labour at Aspull

Henry Meldon, Drawer, Lord Balcarras, Aspall Moor, near Blackrod:

What age are you? – Fifteen nearly.
Do you work in Lord Balcarras's pits? – Yes.
You are a drawer? – Yes, I am, but I am not a full drawer.
What time do you go down in the morning? – I go at five o'clock, and come up at six o'clock at night.
What time have you for meals? – Half an hour for breakfast and one hour for dinner.
Do you work at night ever? – Yes, I work one week at night, and the next in the day-time.
Do you like working in the night? – No. I like the day-time best, but I am like to work at night same as all the rest, or lose my shop.
Are there many little boys in the pit you work in? – Yes, plenty such as him (a little boy of eight or nine years old).
What is his name? – John Church, he works in the same pit as I do.
Have you plenty to eat? – Yes, I get plenty to eat.

Henry Gibson, Drawer at Lord Balcarras's, Haigh, near Wigan, 13 May 1841:

How old are you? – Nearly fifteen.
You are a drawer in one of Lord Balcarras's pits I believe? – Yes, I am.
Are your parents alive? – No. I live with my aunt, and I draw for one of my cousins; I did live with another master but I left him.
Had you clothes given by that man? – No, I had a jacket when I first went to him, but he pawned it.
Do you get any wages from your cousin? – I never draw any myself; my cousin draws my wages, and they gives me meat, and I get enough to eat.
Do they find you clothes? – They ought to do, but I have been a year with them and they have given me none yet; I left them once because they would not give me a pair of clogs and my cousin thrashed me for it.
Did he beat you severely? – Yes, he beat me with a big stick, and the mark is on my arm now (there was a severe bruise on the boy's right arm) and kicked me with his clogs.
What hours do you work? – From five in the morning to half-past five at night.
Do you ever see any other boys beaten by their masters in the pits? – Yes, there is a lad called Jonathan Dicks, from St Helens workhouse, he gets thrashed very ill. I saw his master beat him with a pickaum [arm] on his legs and arms, and his master cut a great gash in his head with a blow of a pick, and he threw a 'cut' at him and swelled up his eye and made it blue.
Are there any other lads who get beaten? – Yes, there is another lad called Andrew, I don't know his other name, he is about eight years old, he comes from Liverpool, and lives with his master, and he is half-clammed [starved], and many a time he comes without any dinner or anything to eat, and we give him some of ours.
(These witnesses could neither of them read or write.)

Evidence given to the Children's Employment Commission (1841)

Two boy miners photographed at the end of the nineteenth century, when the worst excesses of child labour had been eradicated.

## *A Pit Brow Wench for Me*

I am an Aspull collier, I like a bit of fun
To have a go at football, or in the sports to run
So goodbye old companions, adieu to jollity
For I have found a sweetheart, and she's all the world to me.

Could you but see my Nancy, among the tubs of coal
In tucked up skirt and breeches, she looks exceeding droll;
Her face besmear'd with coal-dust, as black as black can be,
She is a pit-brow lassie, but she's all the world to me.

When she turns out on Sunday, now lads, I'll tell you what,
A proper Sunday turn-out, from top to toe she's got;
As fair as any lady – as trim as belle could be,
She is a pit-brow lassie, but she's all the world to me.

Now there is Betty Jenkins, a bonnet she can trim,
She's pretty, and she knows it, although she's rather slim;
But Nancy takes my fancy, a rounded bust has she,
She is a pit-brow lassie, but she's all the world to me.

I never knew such pleasure, before in all my life;
I love my Nancy dearly; she says she'll be my wife;
Her father, too, has gin consent, that married we should be;
She is a pit-brow lassie, and she's all the world to me.

*The Comet* (12 January 1889)

# WHO ELSE WAS AT THE PIT?

Apart from the people we know as 'miners', many other individuals would be involved in a large colliery concern.

Usually a landowner, such as Lord Gerard of Ashton-in-Makerfield, owned the minerals beneath the surface. These he leased to a colliery proprietor or company who had to pay him a certain rent, whether coal was extracted or not. Some landowners, such as the Earls of Crawford at Haigh, were both coal-owners and colliery proprietors. Some colliery proprietors, such as the Blundells of Pemberton, bought estates and became landowners. Colliery owners employed managers or mining agents to be responsible for the day-to-day management of the collieries. Beneath them were the underlookers or foremen and beneath these the firemen who were responsible for safety.

Below the bottom layer of management was an array of skilled craftsmen of various kinds including surveyors, fitters, electricians, joiners, carpenters, wagon builders, blacksmiths, saddlers, painters, signwriters, plumbers, clerks and cashiers, many of whom provided education and training in the form of apprenticeships. In addition there were the occupations more directly connected with the extraction of coal which were included in the blanket term 'miner', such as hewers, pony boys, engine tenters and winders (who were responsible for moving the cages up and down the shafts). A large number of labourers also worked at the pits.

Sometimes there were satellite works involved in processes associated with coalmining such as brickworks and coke ovens. A few colliery companies ran schools for the children of their employees (for example, at Abram).

Meyrick Bankes (1811–81) coal owner and colliery proprietor.

The National Association of Colliery Managers meeting at Wigan, 1899.

Pick sharpeners.

A blacksmith and striker.

A clerk.

Three joiners.

A sawman.

An old labourer transporting logs.

# FROM COAL-FACE TO FIREPLACE

These photographs show the stages by which coal is removed from the coalface and delivered to the customer.
1. Hewers hack coal from the face, and a filler shovels the coal into a tub.

2. A drawer pushes the loaded tub to the bottom of the shaft. (Pit ponies were used later.)

3. The loaded tubs are brought to the surface and a banksman removes them from the cage.

4. Each full tub is weighed on the weighbridge, and the tallyboy calls out the number on the tally (each hewer has a different number) and the clerk makes a note of it. The hewer will be paid according to the number of full tubs he has sent up.

5. The full tubs are moved to the screens. In this case (at Worsley Mesnes Colliery) an endless-chain mechanism is used.

6. The coal is tipped out on to the screens, and the pit-brow women remove any rocks and other rubbish.

7. The coal is transported to the customer. In this case its journey begins by boat.

8. Sometimes the journey is by rail.

9. The coal here is for local domestic use. It is delivered to nearby houses by the coal merchant's horse and cart.

# ACCIDENTS AND DISASTERS

Since 1850, when systematic records began to be kept, over 100,000 people have lost their lives at collieries in Britain. Many of these died in accidents in which they were the only casualty. About half of the victims were crushed by falls of roof.

Only those accidents in which the number of casualties was high came to the attention of the public. As collieries became larger more lives were at risk, and the results of explosions more shocking. Most of these explosions were caused by coal dust or methane. Adequate ventilation was required to dilute inflammable gas. This was done by sinking two shafts, and placing a furnace at the bottom of one of them. As the hot air at the bottom of the upcast shaft rose, fresh air was sucked into the downcast shaft. Later, ventilation was effected by huge fans installed at the top of upcast shafts.

The miner's safety lamp was invented to prevent explosions. Unfortunately the light the early lamps gave off was very weak indeed, and some hewers (who were paid according to piecework) objected to using them. Different manufacturers made their own improvements. The Naylor

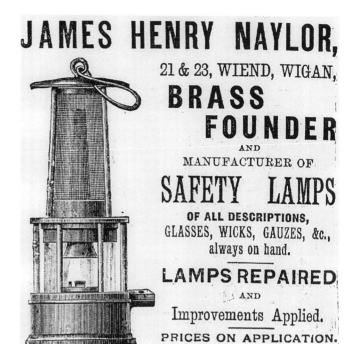

lamp (made in Wigan) had the advantage that the oil could not spill, even if the lamp was tipped up; it could be seen at a glance how much wick was left (thus preventing the lamp going out through lack of wick); it would burn for fourteen hours without the necessity for re-adjustment; and it could be fitted with a unique method of magnetic locking. It had a lighting effect of 1.1 candle power – much more powerful than the early lamps.

Early twentieth-century coalmining rescue equipment.

Thomas Heaton, who invented the miner's electric safety lamp while working as an electrical engineer for the local firm of Pearson and Knowles.

# The Moss Pits Disaster

Like most other mining communities Lower Ince had its fair share of colliery accidents, a particularly serious one being the one that occurred at the Moss Pits of the Pearson and Knowles Coal and Iron Company. This colliery was situated at the end of Cemetery Road, and had only been working a few years when the explosion occurred on Wednesday 6 September 1871. The blast happened in the Wigan 9 ft seam – a notoriously fiery mine. There were about one hundred and fifty men working underground at the time, sixty-eight of them at the 9 ft seam. A loud explosion was heard at the surface, and the ground shook as if by an earthquake, and a dense column of smoke rose from the upcast shaft. The cage was blown to bits and the headgear damaged, but a hoppit (a large iron bucket used for carrying dirt) still hung in the shaft, and this was used to bring up the men who were not working in the 9 ft seam and were uninjured. They were rescued by a party consisting of trade union officials and colliery managers. On approaching the 9 ft seam they found dead and injured colliers lying about, timbers thrown down, and damaged tubs scattered around. The injured were brought up in the hoppit, the rescuers signalling to those above by hitting it with a large hammer. A second, small explosion then occurred, blowing the rescuers several yards down the workings. They were uninjured, however, and managed to make their escape up the shaft, the sides of which were now on fire. It was the unanimous decision of those responsible that any men left alive below could not be saved, and the shafts were capped to stop air getting to the workings, and thus put out the fire. After several days it was assumed that the fire was out, and workmen began to remove the puddling clay and some of the planks from the entrances to the shafts, and then the pit was left for a while to 'ease itself'.

Some time later an exploring party was ready to go down and workmen were beginning to remove the rest of the planks. Thomas Knowles was looking into the upcast shaft, and remarking how quiet things seemed, when there was a sudden rush of wind, flames leaped out of the shaft, and there was a report as loud as that made by a battery of artillery. The engineers and officials at the mouth of the upcast were blown 12 yds on to a railway line, John, the son of Thomas Knowles, receiving a broken leg. The hoppit was thrown up and lodged among the headgear. Four of the workmen were killed, one of them disappearing down the shaft. The sound of the explosion was heard several miles away, and a sheet of flame rose into the air, 20 or 30 ft higher than the top of the headgear. It could be seen from Wigan town centre. Messengers who were sent to run for doctors were delayed as they ran through the streets of Ince, by women and children begging for news, afraid that an explosion had occurred at another pit. A large number of people ran to the colliery and soon the pit banks were crowded with spectators. It was decided to flood the workings using water from the canal, and workmen were busy laying pipes until the early hours of the morning. Later, when everyone had gone home, and the only people around were three policemen, the smoke suddenly increased, and the policemen walked nearer to get a better view. There was another loud report, windows were shaken in villages 4 or 5 miles away, and the policemen ran for their lives with debris falling all around them. Crowds ran to the pit as dawn broke, but it was a dim dawn that morning, because a huge cloud of smoke almost obscured the sun for miles around. At 6.30 a.m. another sheet of fire set the engine house and pit-head gear alight. The Wigan fire-engine arrived at the scene, horses at the gallop, but the water hoses were not long enough to reach the headgear, which collapsed and covered the opening to the shaft. This reversed the ventilation for a few moments, causing smoke to rise from the downcast shaft and the spectators to flee in terror, expecting another explosion. Pumps were brought from other collieries and after about a week of pouring water down the shaft the fire was extinguished.

It took about eight weeks to pump the water out. The bodies that were recovered were identified by their possessions, such as clogs or picks. Eighteen of the corpses were never recovered, and when the colliery began working again, that portion of the mine where they lay remained permanently closed.

On 1 August 1874 a service was held for the dead at the pit head. Revd Thomas Fergie of Christ Church preached an impressive sermon to a congregation of three hundred. Far more came to see the pit burn than came to the service to remember those who died.

# COALMINING HISTORY QUIZ

1. In which year were Britain's collieries nationalized?
2. Which colliery did George Orwell visit to collect information for *The Road to Wigan Pier*?
3. How many men were killed by the Maypole Colliery explosion, Abram, in 1908?
4. How many men were killed in the Pretoria Pit disaster, Westhoughton, in 1910?
5. What were the Protector, the Deflector, and the Thorneburry?
6. When, in the late nineteenth century, a writer in the *Colliery Guardian* wrote that a colliery owner was 'embarrassed in circumstances' what did he mean?
7. What was the name of the colliery locomotive that disappeared down a shaft at Bickershaw on the last day of April 1945?
8. What was special about the ancient coal workings discovered near Arley Hall?
9. What were Bugle Horn, Bull Ring and Cheshire Holes?
10. Who or what were Arthur, Kathleen and Samson?

Do you know the year in which the following collieries closed?
11. Victoria Colliery, Standish.
12. Pemberton Colliery.
13. Worsley Mesnes Colliery.
14. Moss Colliery, Lower Ince.
15. Maypole Colliery, Abram.
16. Wigan Junction Colliery, Abram.
17. Garswood Hall Colliery, Aston.
18. Alexandra Pit, New Springs.
19. Golborne Colliery.
20. Astley Green Colliery.

Do you know the meaning of the following Lancashire coalmining terms?
21. tommy tin.
22. goaf.
23. corve.
24. burgy.
25. banksman.
26. brattice cloth.
27. round coal.
28. step.
29. dataller.
30. outcrop.

(All answers on page 158)

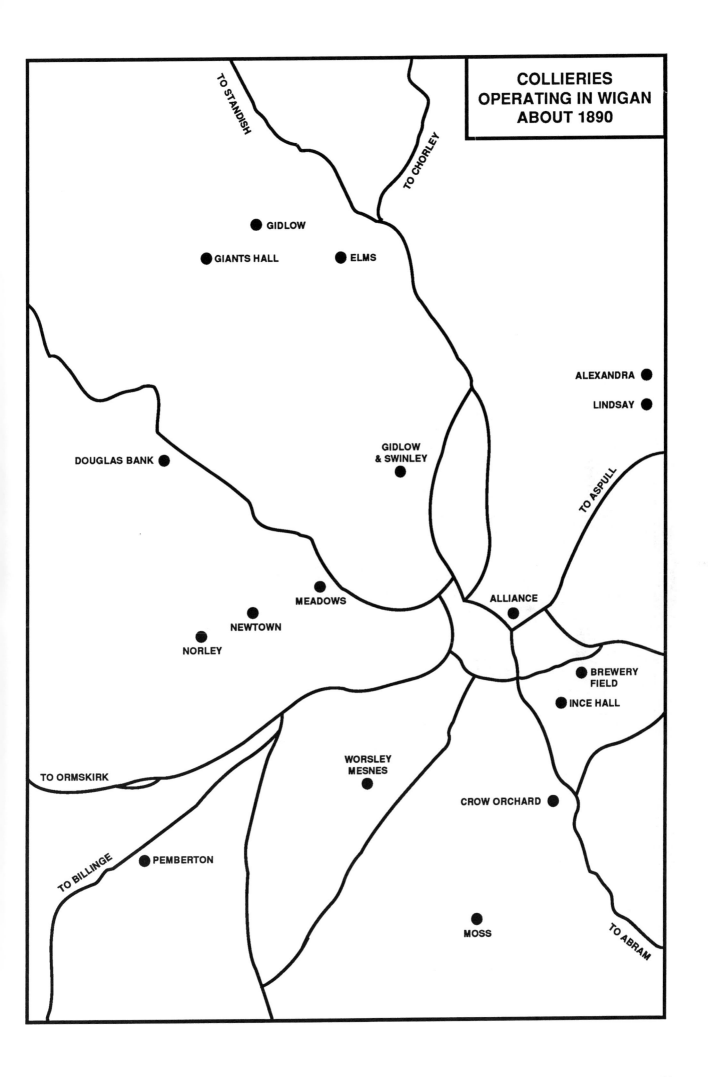

COLLIERIES
OPERATING IN WIGAN
ABOUT 1890

TO STANDISH

TO CHORLEY

● GIDLOW

● GIANTS HALL

● ELMS

ALEXANDRA ●

LINDSAY ●

DOUGLAS BANK ●

GIDLOW
& SWINLEY
●

TO ASPULL

● MEADOWS

ALLIANCE
●

NEWTOWN
●

● BREWERY
FIELD

● NORLEY

● INCE HALL

TO ORMSKIRK

WORSLEY
MESNES
●

CROW ORCHARD ●

TO BILLINGE

● PEMBERTON

●
MOSS

TO ABRAM

# ON THE SCRAP-HEAP

These photographs of the derelict Pemberton Collieries, taken in the 1960s, epitomize the decline of a once great industry.

# INDUSTRIAL UNREST

The coalmining districts used to have a reputation for rioting similar to that of the inner cities today. When trade unions were banned and the vote was denied them the miners backed up their demands with violence against property and people. Working as they did every day in hazardous conditions they were more ready than most to take the risk of becoming involved in a fight with the authorities. Their protests were connected with the trade cycle. When business was good they tried to obtain a pay rise; when it was bad they tried to prevent the employers reducing their wages.

The first miners' trade union in Lancashire was formed in 1794. It was called the Brotherly Union Society, and its members met at the Ben Jonson Inn, in Goose Green. As unions were illegal it operated in the guise of a friendly society.

In 1853 a particularly serious riot occurred in Wigan. The miners had been on strike for several weeks in support of a pay claim, when the employers held a meeting in the Royal Hotel (on the site of John Menzies) to discuss their demands. The town was crowded: the textile workers were also on strike and it was market day and the day of the autumn cattle fair. As the employers left the hotel, the news got around that they had turned down the pay demand. They were jostled and threatened by the crowd, and took refuge in a shop. When the police arrived the crowd attacked them; they fled and barricaded themselves in the police station. The strikers then went on the rampage, breaking into shops and pubs and taking away whatever they could lay their hands on. The mayor sent to Preston for the military but by the time they arrived everyone had gone home.

Another major strike, in 1868, resulted from a trade recession, and an attempt by the employers to reduce wages by 15 per cent. 10,000 of Wigan's 13,000 colliers came out on strike. The employers brought in strike-breakers from other parts of the country. The miners' tactic was for large groups of men from one locality to go to another where they were not known and attack collieries where men were working. 1,500 men attacked the Lindsay Pit, New Springs, drove out the strike-breakers, and occupied the colliery until they were driven off by the military. Gidlow Colliery was attacked by 500 strikers, and the engine house was set on fire.

The bitterest strike, however, was probably that of 1881. The causes were the weakness of the numerous local unions who represented only the better paid hewers; the different demands for which each local union was fighting; and the bitterly cold weather which increased the strikers' suffering. Most of the strikers were unskilled non-union men. Earning low wages and without union funds to support them, their only chance of success was in a short strike. It was this feeling that the strike had to be won quickly that was the cause of much of the violence, from which the unions tried to dissociate themselves.

Apart from pay, one of the main issues was the question

A strike meeting on Wigan Market Square at the end of the nineteenth century.

of the future of the Lancashire and Cheshire Miners' Permanent Relief Society, which was controlled by the employers, but to which the men contributed most of the money. When Parliament passed the Employers Liability Act of 1880, allowing workers to contract out of employers' schemes, the colliery owners threatened to sack any miner who left the Lancashire and Cheshire Society.

For three weeks the south Lancashire coalfield was in chaos, with groups of colliers, thousands strong, moving from one district to another, attacking collieries and strikebreakers, and with the police and military engaging them where they could. There would be other strikes in the future, and the police and military would be called out as a matter of course, but there would be none as violent as this one. A widening trade union membership and an increase in general prosperity took some of the desperation out of the struggle. And the days when Wigan could assemble 10,000 colliers together were to be over before long.

# NOTICE TO THE PUBLIC.

It being reported in various quarters that we, the COMMITTEE and AGENTS of the MINERS' SOCIETY, do acquiesce in the CONDUCT, VIOLENCE and INTIMIDATION now being used by certain parties terming themselves COLLIERS.

We beg leave to inform the PUBLIC at large, that we, the COMMITTEE and AGENTS, disclaim all such CONDUCT, VIOLENCE and INTIMIDATION on our part.

And further, that we CONDEMN all such CONDUCT, VIOLENCE and INTIMIDATION, as we think it detrimental to the interests of society at large, and us as well, and we neither do nor will recognise any Party or Parties using any such Conduct, Violence and Intimidation.

*By order of the COMMITTEE and AGENTS.*

P.S.-We respectfully request all men to refrain from attending such assemblies.

STROWGER, PRINTER, SCHOLES, WIGAN.

A notice issued by union officials dissociating themselves from the acts of violence committed by some strikers.

Some shopkeepers supported the strikers. The notice behind these children queueing at a soup kitchen says that this butcher will peg his prices while the strike lasts.

Strikers maintained the supply of fuel to their homes by picking coal on colliery spoil heaps . . .

. . . or by working outcrops.

Troops in Bolton House Road, Bickershaw, during a coal strike.

Mounted police at Wigan during the General Strike, 1926.

# COTTON MANUFACTURE

The early textile industry was a domestic industry. Machinery such as the spinning wheel, the jenny and the horizontal frame loom was small enough to be accommodated in a cottage, albeit a cottage the design of which had been altered (in the case of cotton weaving) to include a half-basement to house the loom.

Once textile machinery had been invented that required other sources of power than human energy (for example, Arkwright's water frame) then the rise of the factory system was inevitable. The use of the water-wheel to drive the machinery meant that such machinery had to be located near running water (which is why a cotton factory is called a cotton mill). So in Wigan we find the earlier mills such as Acton's Mill and Wood Street Mill (off Chapel Lane), and School Common Mill (at the end of School Lane) all located on the banks of the Douglas.

The application of steam power to cotton manufacture meant that transport became an important factor in determining the location of cotton mills, and we find a cluster of mills (Trencherfield Mill, Swan Meadow Mill, Victoria Mill, etc.) near the canal in Lower Wallgate.

Employment in the Lancashire cotton industry reached a peak in 1912, and then began to decline. Although there was a significant increase in output per employee after the Second World War, this was not able to prevent the virtual disappearance of the industry from Lancashire.

## *The Cotton Masters*

On looking into the origin of the manufacturing firms of this town [Wigan], I find that the masters have, almost to a man, begun with nothing, and risen by little and little, till many of them have got to be very wealthy. One man, Mr William Wood, died in the early part of this year, worth, as stated in the newspapers of the day, £300,000, nearly all of which had been acquired by the factory system.

As men of figures they are often almost without a parallel; they can tell to a nicety how much money will be gained by reducing their hands 6d. per head throughout the factory, or to what the fraction of a farthing per pound or per yard, upon the goods produced, will amount. To their ability in calculating these minute details, may be attributed much of their success as accumulators of wealth.

William Dodd, *The Factory System* (1842)

Cottages specially designed for hand-loom weavers on the site of what is now Swinley Labour Club.

Can you name the mills shown on this page? (Answers on page 158)

# THE FIRST REPORT

OF THE

# THROSTLE HANDS,

## WINDERS & REELERS,

OF THE

# WIGAN UNION.

## Fellow Working Men and Women,

The time is not far distant when the factory operatives of Wigan may receive a fair day's wage for a fair day's work, although it is too well known that the present rate of wages and labour is,---" Plenty to do, and low payment."

The Throstle Spinners, Winders, and Reelers, have now an opportunity of obtaining better wages than they ever received before, if they will only attend to the Rules of their Union, and pay their contributions regularly, in the same good spirit as the people of Stockport and other Towns have done, and where the employers dare not even attempt a reduction of Wages, nor yet refuse to give an advance when fairly and honestly asked for; the operatives in those Towns are so firmly united that they can split assunder the rocks of Slavery, nor suffer themselves to be prematurely buried in their youthful days by the grinding hoof of Capital, and why not the Wigan people free themselves from the yoke of tyranny, and compel their masters to throw off the mantle of deceit, and allow some little comfort to reach the miserable cottage of the Factory Slave?

| INCOME. | L. | S. | D. |
|---|---|---|---|
| Nathaniel Eckersley's Throstle Spinners, Winders, and Reelers | 0 | 15 | 10 |
| (You are good Lasses and like good wags.) | | | |
| Henry Eckersley's Throstle Spinners | 0 | 9 | 6 |
| (Ten per cent. and no surrender!) | | | |
| Messrs. Taylor's New Mill— | | | |
| No. 1 T. Room | 0 | 5 | 6 |
| No. 2 Do. | 0 | 6 | 10 |
| (If that Overlooker does not mind his own business, Punch will say something about him next week.) | | | |
| Do. Reelers and Winders | 0 | 6 | 8 |
| Old Mill— | | | |
| No. 3 T. Room | 0 | 3 | 9 |
| No. 4 Do. | 0 | 2 | 8 |
| No. 5 Do. | 0 | 3 | 4 |
| Do. Reelers | 0 | 3 | 7 |
| Church Street Mill— | | | |
| Bottom T. Room | 0 | 3 | 2 |
| (You are bonny lasses.) | | | |
| Middle T. Room (Shame !) | 0 | 0 | 4 |
| Top T. Room (If they do not pay up, | | | |

| | L. | S. | D. |
|---|---|---|---|
| Punch will say something about them next week.) | 0 | 0 | 3 |
| Ranson's T. Spinners and Reelers (Pay better.) | 0 | 2 | 9 |
| Acton's Throstle Spinners and Reelers | 0 | 4 | 0 |
| Tipping's Old Mill— | | | |
| Throstle Spinners and Reelers (Very good.) | 0 | 5 | 6 |
| (If that little black haired Lass does not pay up this week, Punch will meet her in Scholes the next night she goes again.) | | | |
| John Wood's Throstle Spinners and Reelers | 0 | 4 | 0 |
| Do. Twist Room | 0 | 1 | 3 |
| (If the Jobbers do not pay up to their trade, Punch will let the cat out of the bag next week.) | | | |
| Henry Wood's Throstle Spinners, Winders, and Reelers | 0 | 2 | 10 |
| Eccles's Throstle Spinners and Reelers | 0 | 4 | 6 |
| Johnson's Throstle Spinners and Reelers | 0 | 2 | 9 |
| Rylands' Throstle and Doffers | 0 | 1 | 6 |
| Total | 4 | 10 | 6 |

**N.B.**----The Committee meet on Saturday, at the house of **Mr. Duckworth**, Legs-of-Man Inn, Market-place, from Two o'clock in the Afternoon until Seven, to receive Contributions.

D. THOMAS, PRINTER, MARKET-PLACE, WIGAN.

# IRON AND STEEL

During the eighteenth century iron smelting was carried out by the Earl of Balcarres at the Haigh ironworks in Leyland Mill Lane, using ironstone found in the locality. These reserves were soon exhausted, yet iron smelting became an important industry in nineteenth-century Wigan, because it was found profitable to import ironstone from elsewhere (Furness, for example) and use the surplus small coal from the collieries in the production of iron.

It was for this reason that the Kirkless Coal Company expanded into iron production and built two blast furnaces in 1858. These were the germ of what was to become the largest ironworks in the Wigan district. Two years later the company amalgamated with other local businesses to form the Wigan Coal and Iron Company. By 1873 there were ten furnaces in operation, and in 1889 the company began manufacturing steel. Maximum production was reached shortly before the First World War, but after the war a rapid decline set in. In 1930 the Lancashire Steel Corporation was formed from the Kirkless works, the Warrington works of the Pearson and Knowles Coal and Iron Company, and the Irlam works of the Partington Steel and Iron Company. The Kirkless works were closed down immediately, and nothing now remains of this important industrial complex.

A forge hammer at work.

Kirkless Ironworks.

Worsley Mesnes Ironworks, one of the smaller ironworks, with the disused Worsley Mesnes Colliery in the foreground.

A winding engine, made at the Worsley Mesnes Ironworks, at Moss Hall Colliery in 1905.

# WALKER BROS, ENGINEERS

The largest engineering business to emerge in Wigan was that of Walker Brothers (Wigan) Ltd. It was one of many local firms established during the nineteenth century to supply equipment to the ever-expanding coal mining industry. The firm was set up by one John Scarisbrick Walker at a small foundry off Queen Street in 1866. J.S. Walker had previously been chief draughtsman at the Haigh Foundry, the leading engineering concern at that time and involved with the manufacture of steam winding engines, pumps and so on. His own initial production was much more modest but rapidly expanded especially when two of his younger brothers, Thomas Ashcroft and Edwin Robert, joined him a few years later. The Queen Street premises soon became too small, and it also lacked a railway connection, so in 1873 the firm started to develop a new site west of the town centre, which they christened the Pagefield Ironworks.

Throughout its independent existence the company's output continued to be dominated by orders from mining companies. In particular Walkers specialized in the supply of ventilation equipment and high capacity air compressors, and these products were dispatched world wide. Despite this specialization there was also a willingness to diversify, and this is best exemplified by the creation of a commercial motor department in 1907. The lorries and buses were marketed under the name of Pagefield Motors, and in addition to building conventional lorries, many refuse collection vehicles were produced. The early vehicles all had petrol engines but shortly after diesel engines were introduced in 1930. The company also developed a range of diesel railcars, which sold particularly well in Ireland, Peru and Australia. During the Second World War many thousands of artillery shells were produced together with some marine steam engines for both the naval and merchant fleets.

Although the firm had converted into a limited liability company in 1904, the Walker family, now with second and subsequently with third generation involvement, retained a

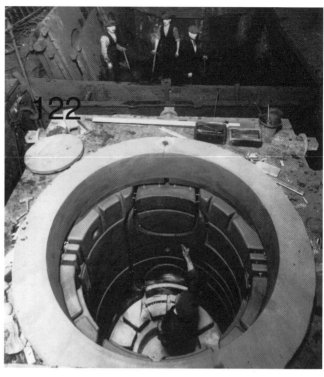

A view inside the foundry at the Pagefield Works, showing work in progress on the casting of a very large cylinder.

controlling interest. The poor trading conditions of the 1930s, together with the ravages of the war years, had taken its toll on the company's finances and in 1946 the works was acquired by Walmsleys of Bury. This company, coincidentally also founded in 1866, had specialized in the manufacture of paper and cardboard manufacturing machinery, and was able to utilize Walker's facilities and skilled workforce to expand their production. Initially the Walker name was retained and their traditional products continued to be built alongside those of Walmsleys origin. By the mid-1950s, however, the mining and vehicle side of the business had been eliminated, and the works continued with the manufacturing of board-making machines until closure in 1983.

An early example of a Walker crane lorry, several versions of which the company produced between 1929 and 1954. This one, seen in the works yard, was supplied to the London Midland & Scottish Railway Co. In the background below the hook can be seen the Douglas Bank signal box, subsequently displayed at the Wigan Pier Heritage Centre.

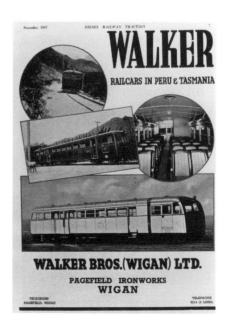

November 1947 advertisement for Walker Brothers diesel railcars, illustrating cars supplied to the Peruvian Corporation (upper) and the Emu Bay Railway, Tasmania, Australia (lower).

A late nineteenth-century external view of part of Walker's Pagefield Ironworks. The small steam locomotive was built by Walkers in 1876 for shunting at their own works and that of the adjacent Wigan Rolling Mills. The large building on the left is the foundry.

A view inside the erecting shops taken at about the same time as the external view above. The machine in the foreground is a two cylinder 'endless-rope' haulage engine, a typical Walker mining product at the time.

During the First World War Walkers supplied over 500 examples of their 'N'-type 3-ton lorry to the War Office for military use. Two examples are seen here on active service close to the front line in northern France.

# ROADS

Archaeological evidence suggests that, with a few exceptions such as Roman roads and motorways, today's pattern of roads, trackways and footpaths originated in late prehistoric times. In the Middle Ages it was one of the duties of a hermit to collect alms for the repair of roads and bridges. From 1555 parishes were responsible for the maintenance of highways. This system proved to be unsatisfactory because the burden of repairing busy roads fell only on the parishes through which they passed. The problem was exacerbated by the significant increase in carriage and cart traffic. A solution was found by allowing groups of businessmen to form trusts that raised capital for road improvements by offering interest rates of about 5 per cent against loans which were repaid from the tolls charged to road users. Tolls were collected by erecting turnpikes or bars across the roads, which were turned to allow traffic through once the fee had been paid.

The Wigan and Preston road had a bad reputation. Cromwell commented on its poor condition when he used it in 1648. It was turnpiked in 1727, but Arthur Young's account (see below), written in 1771, shows what an appalling state it was in at that time.

The location of turnpikes can be determined by place-names (for example, Ince Bar) or by examining the six-inch Ordnance Survey of the late 1840s. This shows, for example, a turnpike on Warrington Road near the present Worthington Way, Hawkley, and one in Wigan Lane at Thorn Hill.

Increasing competition from the canals and railways caused turnpikes to be abandoned in the nineteenth century, the last one closing in 1895.

This iron 'milestone' was one of a number made at Haigh Foundry in 1837.

## DO YOU KNOW?

1. Contrary to popular belief the suffix '-gate' in street names such as Standishgate does not refer to Wigan's medieval town gates. It is derived from the Old Norse 'gata', meaning a road or path. Below are listed some of Wigan's street names that end in '-gate'. Which are authentic, and which date from more recent times?
   Hallgate, Stairgate, Millgate, Marketgate, Wallgate, Bradshawgate (Scholes)
2. Some of the old road-names are no longer in use. What are Highgate and Watergate known as nowadays?
3. What does 'Wiend' mean?
4. What is Robbing (or Robin) Lane called nowadays?
5. What was the alternative name for Poolstock Lane?
6. What was Beggars Walk?
7. What are Higher Gullet and Lower Gullet known as today?
8. Where was Cabbage Lane?

(Answers on page 158)

## The Condition of the Wigan and Preston Road in 1771

I know not, in the whole range of language, terms sufficiently impressive to describe this infernal road. To look over a map, and perceive that it is a principal one, not only to some towns but to whole countries, one would naturally conclude it to be at least decent; but let me most seriously caution all travellers, who may accidentally purpose to travel this terrible country, to avoid it as they would the devil; for a thousand to one that they break their necks or their limbs by overthrows or breaking down. They will meet with ruts which I actually measured four feet deep, and floating with mud only from a wet summer; what therefore must it be after a winter? The only mending it receives is the tumbling in some loose stones, which serve no other purpose but jolting a carriage in the most intolerable manner. These are not merely opinions but facts, for I actually passed three carts broken down in these eighteen miles of execrable memory.

Arthur Young, *A Six Months Tour through the North of England* (1771)

## Tolls to be Paid on the Wigan and Warrington Turnpike Road, 1746

For every Horse, Gelding, Mare, Ass, or Mule, laden with coal or kennel ½d.

For every other loaden Horse, Gelding, Mare, Ass, or Mule ½d.

For every Waggon carrying Coals or Kennel only 6d.

For every Waggon laden with other Goods 1s. 6d.

For every Coach, Berlin, Landau, Chariot, Calash, or Hearse, drawn by Two Horses, Geldings, or Mares 6d.

For every Coach, Berlin, Landau, Chariot, Calash, or Hearse, drawn by Four or more Horses, Geldings, or Mares 1s.

For every Drove of Oxen, Cows, Bullocks, or Meat Cattle, 10d. per Score; and so in Proportion for any greater or less number

For every Drove of Calves, Hogs, Sheep, or Lambs, 5d. per Score; and so in Proportion for any greater or less number

Note the lower rates for the transport of coals and cannel (a high quality coal), showing the importance of these to the local economy.

Pennygate toll bar, Hindley.

# Aspull before the Finger-Post

Today we take for granted the vast number of road signs that have been erected for our convenience. In other days, we may have had to take more trouble, as this traveller relates: 'The park is separated from Aspull Moor by a green lane wearing an antique appearance. We crossed the moor again, passing several large coal pits belonging to the Earl Balcarres, with tram-roads connecting one with the other. The country houses, stone bridges, the wagons – everything is painted of a light blue colour, each bearing in large letters, EARL BALCARRES, No. –.

"Can you" – we asked of a peasant – "can you tell which is the road to Blackrod?"

"Nau" – he replied – "but if ye speer um at yander coal peet happ'n yeell know."

We put the needful questions, and received civil answers.'

– Anon, *Pictorial History of the County of Lancaster* (1844)

Aspull's famous finger post.

Road-widening at Upholland at the beginning of the twentieth century.

Mab's Cross being moved to the other side of the road as part of a road improvement programme, June 1922.

# ROAD TRANSPORT

Medieval roads were very bad and the chief means of transportation was the pack horse. These animals were harnessed with special pack saddles to which baskets or bundles of goods could easily be attached. Pack horses moved in single file, the lead horse wearing a bell or bells to warn other travellers of the approaching train.

During the seventeenth century improved methods of coach and carriage construction resulted in increased traffic, the wheels of which cut up the roads very badly. James Morris of Wigan suggested a wheel with a 13-in face, which would cause less damage, and wide wheels became popular, especially on wagons.

Nationally, the first stage coach began operation on 6 April 1657. By the end of the eighteenth century they could maintain an average speed of between 10 and 12 miles per hour on good roads. The following local advertisement appeared in 1824: 'To MANCHESTER, the *Ancient Briton* from the Buck i' th' Vine [later renamed the Clarence Hotel], every morning at seven (except Tuesday) when it goes at half-past six, – the *Pilot*, from the same inn, every Monday, Wednesday and Saturday afternoon at three and a *Market Coach* from the Commercial Tavern every Tuesday morning at seven.'

The decade from 1820 to 1830 was the heyday of the mail coach, a special fast coach that kept punctually to its timetable, and carried an armed guard. Mail coaches to Liverpool and York called at the Buck i' th' Vine.

The railways put an end to the stage-coach system. For short journeys, however, the horse-drawn omnibus was used. In 1872 omnibus services were operating several times a day from North-West station to Aspull, from the Minorca Hotel to Goose Green, and from the Clarence Hotel to Orrell.

By 1878 the idea of trams in Wigan was being promoted, and on 31 July 1880 the first tramway in Wigan opened with a half-hourly service to Lamberhead Green. However, the gradient was rather steep for horses and by February 1882 steam trams were in operation, although some horse trams continued to run until 1885. By the end of the century the tramways company was in serious financial difficulties and was taken over by Wigan Corporation, who instituted a programme of electrification. At their maximum development Wigan Corporation's tramways ran to Standish, Aspull, Hindley, Platt Bridge, Ashton, Abbey Lakes and Martland Mill. Beyond these termini the Corporation introduced some bus routes (for example, to Billinge and Skelmersdale) but these were later abandoned as unprofitable. In the early 1920s trolleybuses were introduced on some routes, but the future lay with buses, and services were operating to Aspull and the new Beech Hill housing estate in the 1920s. Bus expansion continued: the last tram ran on 28 February 1931 and the last trolleybus on 30 September 1931.

Trippers leaving the Woodhouses Inn by wagonette.

Two of the most important occupations in the days of horse transport were the farrier . . .

. . . and the coachman. Both jobs required a combination of strength, skill and gentleness.

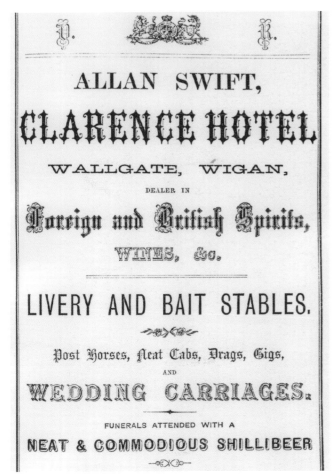

Different types of stabling and various kinds of horse-drawn vehicles are listed on this advertisement for the Clarence Hotel, and include cabs, drags, gigs and a shillibeer.

An early advertisement for Timberlake's. The showrooms were in Library Street.

# THE AGE OF THE TRAM

Wigan's first trams were horse-drawn, but the horses were soon replaced by steam engines. This photograph shows a former horse-drawn car used as a trailer behind a tram engine.

A steam tram, consisting of an engine made by Kitson of Leeds and its bogie trailer, in Ormskirk Road at the junction with Enfield Street.

Electric trams in the Market Place. The double-deckers were originally open-topped, but were enclosed later.

A tower wagon for overhead line maintenance.

Wigan Corporation Transport's fitting shop in 1922, when it employed about twenty men.

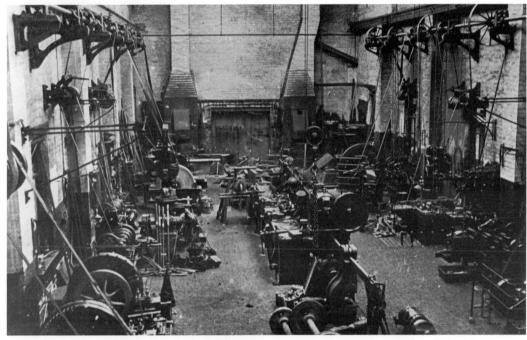

Demolition of the tram sheds in Woodhouse Lane in July and August 1926, after the conversion of the Martland Mill route to trolley buses.

# THE BODY BUILDERS

The interior of William Kenyon and Sons in
Darlington Street.

A horse van made for Henry Atherton and Sons
by William Moss of Orchard Street.

Firms that made bodywork for horse-drawn vehicles
often made the same for motor vehicles. This motor
van body was made by William Moss and Sons.

The manufacture of caravans has long been a speciality of the district, and is continued today by Pemberton Leisure Homes. This horse-drawn touring caravan was made by William Kenyon and Sons of Darlington Street.

This caravan was made by Arkwright's of Goose Green in the 1930s.

The manufacture of public service vehicles continues to be the work of Northern Counties Motor and Engineering Company Ltd, shown here.

# THE RAILWAYS

The practice of transporting material in wagons which ran on fixed rails was already well established when, after the construction of the Douglas Navigation and the Leeds and Liverpool Canal, narrow gauge railways were constructed to carry coal from the pit-heads to the canal. The trains consisted of a few small wagons and were, with one exception, pulled by horses. The exception was Clarke's railway from Winstanley to Crooke, which was worked by Lancashire's first steam locomotive, the Yorkshire Horse, which was made at Haigh Foundry in 1812. In 1832 Wigan had its first public railway when a line was laid from the town to join the Liverpool and Manchester Railway. This line was extended to Preston in 1838.

Further development resulted in Wigan having three railway stations: North-Western, which served lines operated by the London and North-Western Railway; Wallgate, which served lines operated by the Lancashire and Yorkshire Railway; and Central station, which served the Great Central Railway line. Apart from the main lines there were many miles of track used only for industrial purposes.

During the twentieth century a rapidly expanding road transport system proved to be too competitive for the railways, and in 1962 Dr R. Beeching, the head of the new British Railways Board, closed over 5,000 miles of track and 2,000 stations. Wigan emerged relatively unscathed, retaining two of its stations. Central station closed on 2 November 1964.

The railways used to provide employment for thousands of Wiganers, such as these footplatemen.

## Fun and Games on the Wigan and Preston Line

An alarming accident occurred at Wigan on the 26th of August. An excursion train from Morecambe to Manchester broke in two while it was descending the incline to Wigan station, and the rear portion ran into the front portion, which had been brought to a stand. Three persons were injured. The experiences of the driver and his fireman were varied and amusing. The train was a special excursion, of twenty coaches, drawn by a six-coupled goods engine. There was a guard at the front end of the train who could apply Clark and Webb's chain brake to the van and four coaches; there was a guard at the rear end of the train with similar brake power. The driver states that in going up Farrington bank the leading guard put on the brake, and very nearly pulled up the train, without reason. We can imagine how much pleasure this little freak gave a driver doing his best to get up a bank with a heavy train on a wet night. Coming down the incline near Coppul Hall he put the brake on suddenly, and sent the driver and stoker into the corner by the weather board. We are not surprised to hear that the train being thus nearly stopped, the fireman got off the engine to remonstrate with him. The facetious guard told him it was 'all right'. He then let the train run until it had attained a good speed, when he put the brake on again, with the result of rapidly transferring the driver and stoker from one end of the footplate to the other, and then took it off again, with the result that the fireman was jerked over the brake wheel into the coals in the tender. Yet another application, and the train broke in two. The driver expected this would happen, and as soon as the break-away took place he tried to run on ahead, but the indefatigable guard would not have it. He pulled up the train with full steam on, and the rear portion ran into it. Colonel Rich reports on the accident, and states that the guard was not drunk or incapable. The man denied positively that he put the brake on.

*The Engineer* (3 October 1884)

(It was suggested at the inquiry into the accident that the braking mechanism was at fault, and a recommendation made that this type of brake be withdrawn from use.)

The demolition of Central station, 1973.

Evidence of the Great Central Railway's line to Leigh can still be seen in this photograph. The original terminus was here at the junction of Darlington Street and Warrington Lane, before the line was extended and Central station built.

# AGRICULTURE AND FOOD

Agricultural practice in the Middle Ages was based primarily on the cultivation of cereals. The topography, soil, and climate of south-west Lancashire, however, was not really suitable for grain production. Much of the surface area was covered with mossland, and on the higher land the soil was not particularly fertile. In addition the humid climate meant that there had to be a dependence on oats. It was not until most of the mosslands had been drained in the mid-nineteenth century that south-west Lancashire was transformed from a backward agricultural region with low productivity, into one of the most fertile areas of England specializing in the intensive production of vegetables. Wigan, situated at the edge of this fertile zone, and containing a large available labour force, made the town an ideal location for a food-processing plant such as Heinz.

The diet of most of the inhabitants, until the late nineteenth century, was austere. The poor rarely ate vegetables, which, before the days of food processing, could only be obtained in season. The staple fare was potatoes, porridge and jannock. Jannock was a kind of unleavened bread made from oatmeal. It remained edible for several weeks after baking. Even into the twentieth century those foods associated with Lancashire – tripe, black peas, and meat pies – were identified with poverty.

It used to be the custom for Wigan publicans, at a certain time of the year, to bake large potato pies in each of which a small earthenware doll was placed. When the pie was cut up, whoever had the doll bought a round of drinks for the other diners.

As most houses in towns did not have gardens some people, such as this old man, supplemented their diet by growing vegetables on allotments.

There are two interesting facts connecting Wigan with the history of food production. The earliest surviving record of the retail sale of potatoes occurs in the Michaelmas Court Leet records of 1680; and one of the greatest orchard nurseries on record (that is, in the number of varieties offered) was established in Wigan by William Pinkerton in the late eighteenth century.

This photograph of Birchley Hall Farm at the beginning of the twentieth century shows how labour intensive food production was at that time.

Sutton Mill, a water-powered corn mill at the bottom of Coppull Lane. Mills such as this had been grinding corn in Britain since the Roman era.

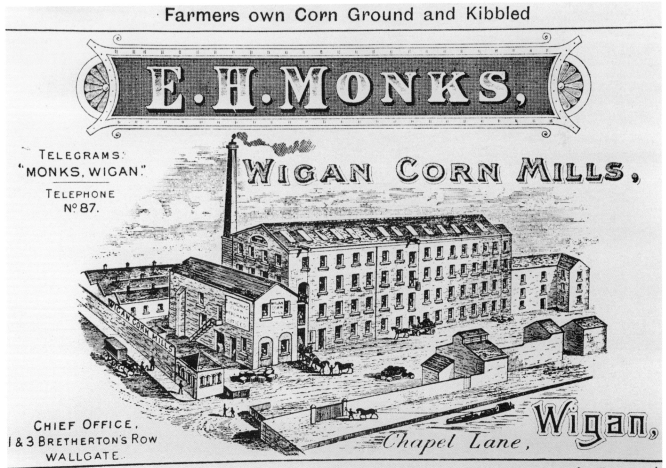

The introduction of steam power affected agricultural as well as industrial production. E.H. Monks' steam-powered corn mills were sited, like cotton mills of the same period, beside the canal to facilitate transportation.

# Problems with Porridge

I remember another story which was to my grief . . . that the world may see what straits I have been in, and what troubles I have undergone in my life. When I lived with Mr Livesey, he sent me to High Leigh to Mr Henry Lee about a minister for his chapel, and going from Budworth to High Leigh without victuals I came just at dinner time. Mr Lee was at dinner. I sent letter to him: he sent word I should stay dinner, which I did, and was very hungry. I was set at table with servants. Every servant a great bowlful of porridge, anon a great trencher like a pot lid I and all the others had, with a great quantity of porridge. The dishes elsewhere but small and few. I put bread into my porridge, thinking to have a spoon, but none came. While I was thus in expectation of that I could not obtain, every man having a horn spoon in their pockets, having done their porridge, fell to the other dishes. Thought I, these hungry Amalekites that I am gotten amongst will devour all if I do not set upon a resolution. . . . Well, I resolved; 'Hodge, if thou will have any victuals here, thou sees how the case is, and into whose company thou art fallen into, what a hungry spirit possesses these men'; and a speedy dispatch with the porridge accordingly I did, and sweeped it as if I would have drunk. Then, when I had it in my mouth I was in such a hot fit in my mouth as turned meditation into action, but at last, to my lamentation, I was worse than before. I would gladly have given five shillings that I but had the benefit of air or a northern blast of wind. My tongue in my mouth was in a sad condition; help myself I could not, for the table was before me and a wall behind me upon my back, a woman with her basket upon my right hand, and a man with his cod piece upon the other, and in this sad condition I sat blothering, knew not what to do best. That little porridge I tasted was both dinner and supper. I at last rose from the table with a hungry belly but a lamenting heart, and ever since I have been cautious how to sup porridge, and likewise wary. Nothing worser to a man than over hastiness, especially in hot concernments.

*Diary of Roger Lowe of Ashton-in-Makerfield*
(13 October 1663)

# Infants Food

Take a pound of the best flour, tie it *very tightly* in a strong cloth, and put it into a pan of boiling water (in which put a plate, to prevent the cloth sticking to the bottom of the pan). Boil it for three hours without allowing it to go off the boil, – when coldish untie the cloth, and scrape off the outside of the ball: when to be used, grate down the quantity required, and break it with cold water; boil four or five minutes only, and sweeten to the taste. Flour prepared in this way is confidently recommended by an experienced sick nurse as a soft and nutritious food for the youngest infant, and will keep for a month or more in its hard, compact state. Milk may be added when about to be eaten, if wished.

*Wigan Observer* (January 1853)

Although commercial bakeries have existed since the Middle Ages, the baking of bread was still a common domestic activity in the nineteenth century. Sometimes outside bread ovens were used, as shown here.

An early twentieth-century commercial bakery at Golborne.

# HYGIENE AND PUBLIC HEALTH

The health of any community is dependent upon an adequate supply of clean water, and an efficient method of disposing of sewage.

As the population of towns grew the system of wells became inadequate, and reservoirs were built to provide an adequate water supply. In the eighteenth century Wigan had a reservoir in Coppull Lane. The date of its construction is unknown, but it may have been earlier than the Whitley Reservoir which was made in 1764. Wooden piping was used (some of this was discovered in Wigan Lane in 1930) until cast-iron piping was introduced in the late eighteenth century. Rural areas had to wait until much later for a piped water supply (Standish received piped water in 1892).

In the 1840s a series of reports was produced on sanitation in Wigan. These were part of a wider national concern with public health. The reports showed the inhabitants of the town living in unbelievable filth. In this Wigan was no different from other towns of the period. A sewage system was laid out in the 1850s, the effluent being deposited in the River Douglas to the west of the town.

As far as personal health was concerned, people relied upon the efficacy of prayer, the curative powers of mineral waters, and traditional or quack remedies. In the Middle Ages, Wigan had a 'holy well' which later became, in the eighteenth century, Wigan Spa (near the site of the present police station). Traditional remedies, ranging from the bizarre to the disgusting, were passed on from generation to generation. In Wigan Archives there is a notebook, of about 1820, which contains a 'cure' for tuberculosis consisting of coal-dust mixed with milk. Newspapers advertised quack remedies and cure-alls.

Perhaps the best recipe for good health was that given by Ralph Standish in the eighteenth century, when he wrote: 'Eat moderately hot meals: the best Physic is warm clothes, warm diet, and a merry, honest wife.'

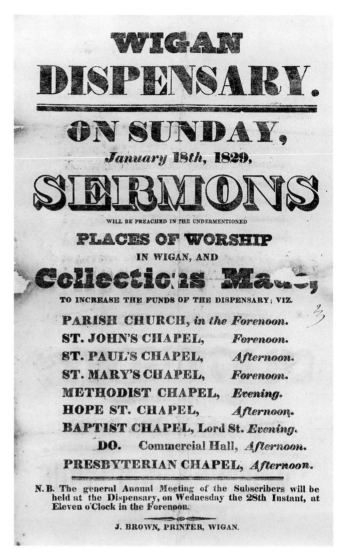

Medical establishments often had no reliable and regular source of income, but were dependent on appeals to the public. Collections were often made in factories and churches.

## Wigan Spa

Wigan Spa or New Harrogate is a strong sulphurous water, lately discovered in boring for coal in a field near the Scholes Bridge; it is said to greatly resemble the water of Harrogate in Yorkshire, only that it does not contain as much saline matter as that does; it contains a considerable quantity of very fine sulphur, and has been found useful in most complaints for which sulphur waters have been recommended; it has been made use of in a variety of complaints, and frequently with good effect: amongst others the following may be particularly mentioned: sore eyes, particularly those of long standing; old sore legs and other old sores; scald heads; the scurvy, itch and many other eruptions or cutaneous complaints, scrofulous sores etc; in all these disorders patients have frequently been known to obtain a perfect cure by use of this water. There is now a very elegant building erected for the use of those who resort to this spring, with convenience for drinking the water, and for using it either as a hot or cold bath.

*The Travellers Companion* (1788)

# Factory Cripples

There is a great number of factory cripples by accident, and long hours of labour, in Wigan; my guide had run over the names of thirty or forty in a short time. A few cases I shall lay before your Lordship: those having friends in the mills were not willing to let me have their cases, as it might give offence, if it came to the ears of the manufacturers.

MARY BROWN, a young woman about twenty-three years of age, was attending a throstle-frame in Messrs JOHNSON and AINSWORTH's cotton factory, in November, 1839, and was cleaning the machine while it was going (as she was not allowed to stop it for that purpose), about four o'clock in the afternoon. She was so unfortunate as to get her left arm in among the wheels, just above the wrist, by which both bones in the fore-arm were broken, the flesh dreadfully crushed and lacerated, and the hand almost severed. Her hand is stiff and contracted, the wrist immoveable. She gets a scanty living by selling cakes, &c. Her masters, who are wealthy, have done very little for her.

WILLIAM SAYER lost his right arm, a few inches below the shoulder, in the scutcher in Messrs ACTON and ROBY's mill. The firm is rich, but I cannot learn that they have done anything for him. He is about twenty-four years of age, and stands six feet high. His sight is very much impaired; he is endeavouring to pick up a living by attending on the market-people.

EDWARD LEATHERLAND, a young man about nineteen years of age, lost his right arm in the scutcher in WILLIAM WOOD's factory. He has received nothing from his masters, and is endeavouring to gain a living by gathering manure in the streets. He lives with his parents, who are very poor.

HENRY ROBINSON lost his right arm in the scutcher in Messrs ECKERSLEY and SON's factory. He now goes with a boat on the canal: his masters have done a little for him.

ESTHER TOPPING lost her left hand in WILLIAM WOOD's factory. She has not been in any way provided for, is not able to get a living, and is now assisting her mother who is very poor.

These cases of accidents will show your Lordship the necessity of machinery being well boxed-off, which, generally speaking, is not the case.

William Dodd, *The Factory System* (1842)

# Farrington and Son's False Limbs

A Wigan coal and Iron Co.'s official recently sent his daughter to Farrington and Son's, of Wigan Lane, Wigan to have an artificial leg made to order, and after only one quarter of an hour's exercise the lady was able to walk to the railway station without any assistance; and every evening the following week was able to take cycling exercise whilst wearing the artificial leg and in ordinary boots. She also recently called on the makers and showed the splendid qualities of the limb by riding the cycle in Wigan Lane to the amazement of many who were acquainted with the case. Name of above given if desired.

*Wigan Observer* (12 August 1899)

The loss of life or limb was a risk the coalminers faced each day.

# Cholera at Marsh Green

Mr Thicknesse asked what was doing with regard to Marsh Green? – The Clerk stated that he had given directions to the officer to take any steps he might think proper, and a house was to be taken for the reception of cholera patients.

Mr Thicknesse suggested that thorough whitewashing was wanted, and that there were many filthy holes which should be filled up.

The Clerk said that there was one thing – though he did not know whether he should apply to Mr Bevan publicly about it. It was said that the people of Marsh Green were short of water for household purposes, and that they could get good water from Mr Bevan's land. He wished to know whether Mr Bevan would lay down a tile drain from the source?

Mr Bevan said it would be more than 15 acres across the estate. When he first took the property he found the inhabitants trampling the land all over for water. He made them a very easy access for water, putting down steps, and telling them that they were at perfect liberty to fetch the water, only they must keep on the footpath. He made everything as convenient as possible, and the water was so pure he could drink it himself.

The Clerk suggested that Mr Bevan should drain his land and make a reservoir.

Mr Bevan did not know where to drain from. He wished to do everything for the benefit of the neighbourhood. So far he regarded the little property he had at Marsh Green, he wished to get the tenants out of it. He gave the proper notice for some of the tenants to go, and before they went they cut the fruit trees and destroyed the plants, although he told them he would pay for everything they left on the property.

The Clerk said that perhaps Mr Harrison had better wait upon Mr Bevan privately, and explain.

Mr Bevan expressed his opinion, that so far as regarded water, the people would be too idle to fetch it, if it were provided.

Mr Acton, understanding the people to be in such a state of destitution, thought it advisable that the relieving officer should have a stock of blankets at Marsh Green.

The Clerk suggested that they should make arrangements with the party who furnished the blankets in Wigan. A number had been taken to Hindley on the understanding that those not required should be returned.

*Wigan Times* (7 September 1849)

# Owd John's Tooth

Owd John was a well-known character in nineteenth-century Parbold and the following story is told about him:

On one occasion John was troubled with tooth-ache, and adopted the following drastic measure for the removal of the offending molar: 'Betty and me had gone to bed one neet, and th' tooth started a wortchin worse nor ever, so aw geet up and went down steers into th' kitchen. And after aw'd gotten th' tooth eawt, aw went up to bed again, and eawr Betty says, "John, eaws thi tooth na?". "Well," I says, "Betty, if tha wants to know tha mun go an ax it, th' tooth's on't kitchen dresser, I hove it eawt wi' a three-pronged fork."

William Price, *Some notes on the places, traditions, & folklore of the Douglas Valley*

## Lack of Sanitation in Hallgate

Top Croft and Lower Croft in Hall-gate, returned as seats of fever, are, on the whole, the worst cottage property in the town. The filth from the houses and privies of Upper Croft drains over an unpaved surface into an open ditch, which runs along the back of the houses of the Lower Croft. This ditch is about 3 feet above the floor of the houses, and its contents ooze through the walls, and in wet weather overflow into the windows. Beamish, a weaver, works in one of these cellars. The wood work is rotten, and the bed clothes in the room above are much affected by the damp. In another room, unpaved, the loom-treadle is placed in a hole, and this is occasionally flooded. The cases are numerous in which these cellar weaving-shops are injuriously affected by putrescent filth.

G.T. Clarke, *Report to the General Board of Health*
(1849)

This photograph of the unpaved and undrained Millstone Yard in Wigan Lane shows the insanitary conditions some Wiganers were living in about 1900.

# COUNTY BOROUGH OF WIGAN.

## SMALLPOX.

This loathsome and fatal disease is prevalent in this country at the present time. The only way to protect yourself is to be vaccinated. Look at these illustrations and then decide to get vaccinated at once.

It can be done by any doctor or free of cost by a public vaccinator.

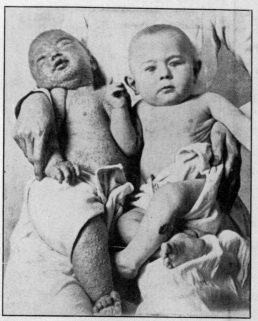

This is a reproduction of a photograph of two children in an Isolation Hospital. The one on the left was unvaccinated and had smallpox. The other infant was admitted with its mother who was suffering from smallpox, and was vaccinated on admission. He remained perfectly well with his mother in the Hospital, while the unvaccinated child died.

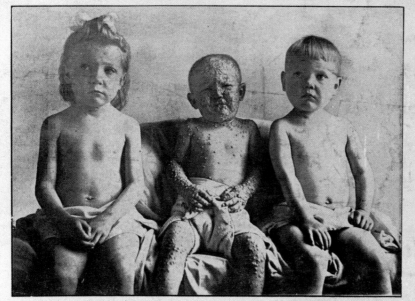

This illustration is from a photograph of three members of a family brought to an Isolation Hospital with their mother who was suffering from smallpox. The child in the centre was unvaccinated, the other two had been vaccinated the year before. The two vaccinated children remained in the smallpox wards several weeks and never contracted the disease.

Unless you have been successfully vaccinated against smallpox during the last five years, do not delay.

## GET VACCINATED
## NOW.

In spite of increasing malnutrition among the children of the unemployed, advances were made in infant health during the inter-war years. This healthy-looking baby is at Leigh Child Welfare Clinic.

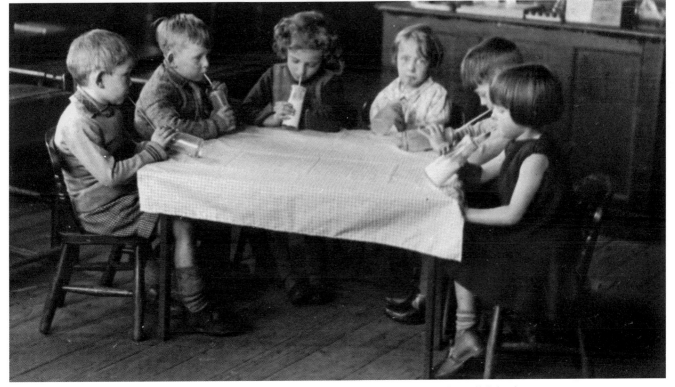

Free school milk often helped to improve an inadequate diet. These children are at Crooke Council School.

# HOUSE AND HOME

When Wigan became a borough each burgess was granted a strip of land (with an end facing on to one of the main streets) on which to build his house. As the burgesses were wealthier than the other inhabitants, Wigan's Market Place and main streets were lined with the more impressive houses in the town. Even the local rural gentry such as the Dicconsons of Wrightington and the Gerards of Ashton-in-Makerfield had their 'town houses' in Wigan.

By the late eighteenth century Wigan was industrializing, and the population was expanding rapidly. The burgesses began to build rows of cheap cottages on their burgage strips, and to build new houses for themselves in the more salubrious area of Wigan Lane. During the latter half of the nineteenth century the houses in these yards came to be inhabited by the poorest section of the town's population, especially Irish immigrants. More solid rows of terraced houses were built for the working class, especially in Whelley, Newtown and Ince. Swinley developed as a mainly middle-class suburb, with the larger houses facing on to the major roads such as Kenyon Road and Bridgeman Terrace, and the smaller houses in the side-streets.

By the beginning of the twentieth century Wigan was suffering from a chronic housing shortage and many houses were unfit for human habitation. The first council houses were built on the Beech Hill estate, which was bought by Wigan Borough Council in 1922. Economic depression and world war delayed progress, however. Scholes, the largest area of sub-standard housing, was redeveloped in the late 1960s. The 1991 census showed that Wigan Metropolitan Borough had approximately 70 per cent owner-occupiers, 24 per cent council tenants, and 5 per cent tenants of other landlords.

*DO YOU KNOW?*
Who was known as the 'Human Mole'? (Answer on page 158)

Saracens Head Yard, Wigan Lane (near the junction with Coppull Lane) showing cheap housing built on a burgess strip.

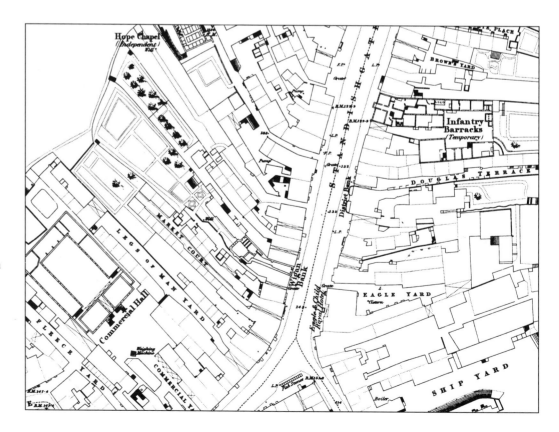

Part of an Ordnance Survey plan published in the 1840s showing burgage strips in-filled with housing. Remnants of the formal gardens laid out when Standishgate was occupied by wealthy citizens can be seen opposite Hope Chapel.

96

# A Club Row Scene

TOWN HALL, FRIDAY
*Before the Mayor and Justice Aspinall.*

Joseph Worrell and his wife preferred a charge against Mrs Ann Bates (who was possessed of a very cunning sken in her eyes) for creating a tumult and disturbing the neighbourhood continually, by standing opposite Worrell's domicile and making use of the most vile and unladylike expressions towards Mrs Worrell.

Magistrate: Well, Joseph, now tell us what all this disturbance has been about.

Joseph: Please, Your Worship, I can't sit quietly at my loom without Mrs Bates coming and abusing us most shamefully. (Mrs Bates now cast a venomous squint at Joseph.) Last Wednesday she called me a duck-stealer and all types of rogues, thieves, robbers and rascals, as ever she could lay her precious tongue to. She says to my wife, says she –

'It isn't his wife', vociferated Mrs Bates; 'it's only his tally-woman; and by leave of your worship –'

Magistrate: Speak when your turn comes, Mrs Bates; we must have one at a time.

Joseph then proceeded: 'It's a nice thing', says she to my wife, says she, 'It's a nice thing for you to wear your stolen cap and bedgown; you look capital in it, by my soul, you do, you nasty, dirty', – (Here followed some of the most elegant names which can be picked up from the lingo of Club Row; and at the recital Mrs Bates looked on both sides of the room at once). It's the first time I ever was at law, Your Worships, said Joseph, and it's only for the peace of the neighbourhood.

James Hastings, a neighbour, said that Mrs Bates was always raising a molesteration in the street with Mr and Mrs Worrell; and when she does that she rises other people in the discourse.

'There it is', said Mrs Bates, 'they're in a conspiration, Your Worship, to bring me in guilty.'

John Willis, another neighbour, said that Mrs Bates had frequently charged Mrs Worrell with being in the family way, and when in that state she took a great many combustibles of all sorts. (This caused much merriment in the court.) The neighbours could not live peaceable, and were unable to bring up their children in a Christianable manner, her discourse was so bad.

The defendant began her story by telling the bench that Mrs Worrell called her Thompson's Grey Mare, and used to tell her children to go home and ask their mother what red-headed bull was their father. (laughter). She also called her Skenning Nance. Wasn't that shameful?

Willis was again called, and said that no such words were used by Mrs Worrell on Wednesday, but the bad language of Ann Bates would fill a newspaper.

Mrs Bates then commenced another long yarn, but the Bench interposed, and put an end to the Club Row scene by ordering Mrs Bates to pay 4s. 6d. expenses. The parties then made their exit.

*Wigan Gazette* (14 April 1837)

(Club Row was a euphemism for working-class housing)

Single-storey, thatched cottages such as these in Hindley were common before the industrial revolution. In the background looms the headgear of Ladies Lane Colliery.

Little London, an area of slum housing was built next to, and behind, middle-class housing in Standishgate. This promiscuous mixing of housing for different classes was typical of the pre-industrial town and sometimes led to friction. See *A Gentleman's Complaint* (below).

## A Gentleman's Complaint

Sir – through the medium of your *Mirror* I would wish to call the attention of the Borough Constables (or those whose duty it is) to try if they cannot put an end to the trick, now so prevalent among the lower class, of impudently seating themselves upon the steps of gentlemen's houses. A company of them congregate together, and will scarcely move for you to walk into your house; and not only so, but their conversation, which may be generally overheard, is very opprobrious. Of the truth of this, I doubt not, you will have had ocular demonstration: and should any means be adopted to put a stop to this piece of impudence, I am sure the ladies of Wigan will be very much obliged.

Letter to the *Wigan Mirror* (15 July 1825)

Swinley Road at the end of the nineteenth century. Landowners leased their land to small businessmen who built a few houses at a time, which resulted in piecemeal development.

The Elms, Wigan Lane. The house and land were bought by Wigan Corporation in 1923 to prevent speculative builders from spoiling the landscape. It was later absorbed into Wigan Infirmary.

Crawford Terrace, a typical street in old Scholes, was situated behind houses in Greenough Street.

The demolition of old Scholes. This photograph is of Gaskell Street.

The clearance of the older over-crowded areas of the town meant that many people were re-housed on the outskirts of the borough. These council houses are at the former hamlet of Marsh Green.

Building has continued in the Wigan Lane area, but tree preservation orders and similar regulations have helped to preserve the sylvan atmosphere. This is The Hollies.

# MARKETS AND SHOPS

*DO YOU KNOW?*

In 1885 M. Connolly had a stall in Wigan market and was advertising 'Blue Points and East Rivers of the best quality', and 'Dutch Natives to be had during the season'. What was he selling? (Answer on page 158)

The Anglo-Saxon king of England Edward the Elder (900–25) decreed that all buying and selling should take place openly in a market-place and within the jurisdiction of a town reeve. Gradually fairs emerged as more seasonal gatherings than markets (which were held weekly), drawing in traders from more distant parts. During the period of the Norman kings charters granting the receipt of tolls and fines (for the breaking of market regulations) were issued by the crown, to which the towns paid a fee for the privilege. The greatest proliferation of such grants occurred during the thirteenth century, and it was during this period that Wigan was granted the privilege of holding markets and fairs. The markets were originally held in the market-place, of course, and not only goods but also livestock was sold. In 1877 a new market hall was built and a market square laid out, and the sale of goods separated from that of livestock. At this time there was, during the week before Easter, a cattle fair on Wednesday, a horse fair on Thursday and a toy fair on Good Friday. There was a combined horse, cattle and toy fair held on the third Wednesday and Thursday in October. Scholes had its own fair on 27 June.

Shops, in the sense of places selling goods that had been produced elsewhere, had been established in Wigan at least from the beginning of the seventeenth century. The late nineteenth century saw the establishment of high-class department stores selling a wide variety of goods. The popularity of the private car in the late twentieth century resulted in the establishment of supermarkets on the outskirts of the town.

A photograph of the market being held in the Market Place sometime before the Market Hall was opened in 1877.

The fish market or fish stones. Stalls for fish were usually made of stone. Although the ones in Wigan appear to have been made of wood, they were still known as The Fishstones.

Wigan Market Hall shortly before its demolition. Public concern that it would be replaced by an ugly modern shopping precinct proved to be unfounded.

A busy scene on Wigan Market Square, which was situated next to the Market Hall.

Turning the front room of one's house into a shop could be a way of supplementing one's income. This was Miss Thomas' Toffee Shop in Standishgate.

A typical corner shop, this was Sherrington's in Scholes. Such shops fulfilled the role of little community centres, and offered credit when times were hard.

Latimer's shop staff, 1952. In the days before supermarkets the customer told the assistant what he or she wanted, and the assistant went and took it off the shelf.

As most people did not own cars in which to bring home their week's shopping, large grocery stores would employ delivery boys, who delivered the purchases by bicycle.

A typical locally owned department store catering for the more affluent customer. Such shops were sometimes given impressive names associated with royalty or the aristocracy. Pendlebury's Crawford House in Standishgate was another example.

Michael Marks, co-founder of the firm of Marks and Spencer, was a Jewish immigrant from Poland who began his working life as a poor hawker in Leeds. As he did not speak English very well and was unable to haggle, he put all his goods in open baskets, together with the notice 'Don't ask the price – It's a penny'. Marks had hit on a successful retail formula, for the customer did not like haggling either. Marks established several stalls in Wigan Market Hall. In 1894 Tom Spencer, a cashier, went into partnership with Marks. In 1899 the company acquired its first leasehold property – at the bottom of the Makinson Arcade (shown here).

Marks and Spencer's department store in Standishgate at the time of its opening.

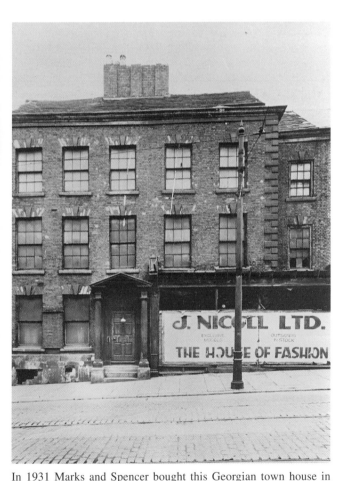

In 1931 Marks and Spencer bought this Georgian town house in Standishgate and built a modern store on the site. Within a short time the company had transformed itself from a business that sold small, cheap goods to poor people, to a national retail chain that sold a variety of goods, with the accent on quality.

# LOCAL GOVERNMENT

Until the granting of the charter in 1246 Wigan was administratively indistinguishable from many other parts of the area described in Domesday as 'Between Ribble and Mersey'. From then on, with its own guild merchant, market, fairs and courts, Wigan developed quite distinctly from the surrounding parts of what is now the Wigan Metropolitan Borough.

Until 1834 the manorial court leet was the principal institution for administration and justice, and since most of the rectors were absentees the burgesses gained control of the court from early on. By the seventeenth century the full range of borough officials had emerged, and these continued until the reforms of the 1830s. The town had a mayor (chosen annually), clerk, bailiffs, surveyors of flesh and fish, searchers, sealers and registerers of leather, ale-tasters, serjeants to keep order, gate-waiters to report on 'strangers' entering the town and to make presentments to the courts, toll-takers and treasurers.

Wigan's government was in the hands of its burgesses, many of whom, such as the Markland family which held the mayoralty ten times between 1623 and 1742, were tradesmen and merchants. They originally held from the rector burgage tenements of $1\frac{1}{4}$ acres at an annual rent of 12d., and retained power up to the nineteenth century by electing themselves and their friends at the court leet. The ordinary citizen had no democratic rights. The Municipal Corporations Act (1835) specified that in towns such as Wigan the previous *ad hoc* arrangements should be replaced by a standard type of constitution. The town henceforth had a corporation comprising councillors (elected by ratepayers and representing defined areas called wards), aldermen and a mayor, who supervised the work of paid officials through meetings of the council and its committees. The concept of a council as we understand it today was born. However, there was much continuity between the old corporation and the new, and little real change in the type of men who ran the town for many decades after 1835.

In Victorian times local authorities such as Wigan became responsible for more aspects of public life. The council had its own police force and acted as a Board of Health. Many new committees were created and Wigan became a county borough in 1888 with the same powers as the new county councils. As the population expanded so did the need for essential services such as lighting, power, streets and pavements, water, sewerage and cleansing, markets and public transport. Education became a borough responsibility under the 1902 Act.

In 1877 Wigan was able to open and subsequently expand one of the finest provincial libraries in England, thanks to the generosity of mill owner Thomas Taylor and a surgeon, Joseph Winnard. The Market Hall (1877), Mesnes Park (1878), and, albeit later than neighbouring towns, a small public baths (1882), were other notable council works. The council continued to expand its role after the First World War, especially in public housing. By the 1960s it was redeveloping the town, building new houses, roads, schools, shopping precincts, car parks, and in 1966 probably the crowning glory of the old county borough, Wigan International Pool.

Finally, in 1974 Wigan was combined with Leigh Municipal Borough and the surrounding district councils to form one of the new Metropolitan Boroughs under the general reorganization of English local government.

> *DO YOU KNOW?*
> 1. Who or what were the Wigan Waits?
> 2. Until at least the 1920s Wigan Corporation employed an officer whose duties included looking after lost children. What was his official title?
> 3. Why would you think twice before you got into an argument with one of Wigan's burleymen?
>
> (Answers on page 158)

Wigan's first charter of 1246 has not survived, but a verbatim account of it appears in this charter of Edward II, granted in 1314.

Surprisingly, Wigan did not have an official coat of arms until 1922. Before this date the badge shown here, the design of which was based on a seventeenth-century town seal, was used as a substitute.

# The Moot Hall and the Town Halls

Wigan has had four known seats of local government. The first was the Moot Hall, which was situated at the Wallgate entrance to the Market Place. The second was the Corporation Hall, situated in the Market Place. The third was the Town Hall in King Street. The fourth is the Town Hall (formerly the Wigan Mining and Technical College) in Library Street.

The origins of the Moot Hall are lost in obscurity. It is not mentioned in Wigan's first royal charter, which merely states that the burgesses may have a guild merchant and a treasury. We do not know how long it was before they had a separate building to meet in. The first surviving mention of the Moot Hall dates from the fifteenth century. A seventeenth-century town seal has a representation of the Hall. It shows a hip-roofed building standing on rows of four pillars, with a door in the middle opening on to a balcony. On the ridge of the roof is a belfry containing the market bell and in front of the Hall is shown a market cross on a flight of three circular steps. On the roof is a sword (presumably to show that justice was administered there) and a flag-pole with a flag flying. It was usual, in such buildings, for the ground floor to be occupied by traders, and we know that in 1598 there were butchers' shops under the Hall. In 1652 the Corporation ordered that 'all the charters, evidences, writeings and munimentes which do concerne the toune' should be stored in the Moot Hall in a purpose-made chest with three locks. The mayor, town clerk and bailiff were each to have a key. It was further ordered that the recorder 'shall twyce every yeare . . . att Michaelmas and Easter Leetes in open court reed the said charters in the English tongue, to the end of the burgesses of this burrowe may be enabled to know there privileges'.

In 1719 the Moot Hall practically fell down and was rebuilt by the rector. The Corporation, however, had themselves a new town hall built in the Market Place. It was paid for by the town's two MPs, the Rt Hon. the Earl of Barrymore, and Sir Roger Bradshaigh. The cost was over £2,000. It was a two-storeyed building, the ground floor being occupied by butchers' shops and known as the Shambles. On the first floor was the council chamber. A railed balcony was added later. On the roof was the royal coat-of-arms carved in stone. In 1862 the Borough Surveyor reported to the Corporation and the occupants of the shops that the building was unsafe and ought not to be made use of unless repaired. In 1882 it was demolished.

The Moot Hall was demolished and rebuilt in 1829. The *Wigan Herald* reported on 21 August: 'The new Moot or Market Hall is fast completing, and presents a plain stone front with colonnade underneath; it is a great pity that its projection on the entrance to the Market Place could not have been obviated.'

And on 9 October: 'The new Moot Hall presents a very handsome frontage . . . The piazza in front already exhibits a neat and elegant shop opened in the tea and grocery trade by Mr Rigby. The architect must correct one fault of this building, perceptible in the interior: we allude to the sound of carts etc., being gathered under the piazza and, from the open construction and position of the entrance door and staircase, interrupting the business of the court: the railing at the top of the staircase should be closed up and a close folding door put up as well to prevent this noise as to keep the court sufficiently warm.'

J. Rigby's grocery shop was one of the most fashionable in town. In 1829 he specialized in tea and coffee, selling 16 kinds of Chinese tea with such names as Twankay, Fine Twankay and Curled Leaf Twankay.

The new Moot Hall was quite unsatisfactory, and as early as 1852 there were calls for its demolition. Eventually the building was demolished in 1869. The *Wigan Observer* of 21 August 1869 reported: 'The Moot Hall was sold by auction yesterday. Messrs Lamb and Sons were the auctioneers. There was a very large attendance, and the lots realized good prices. The conditions of sale require the taking down of the building in six weeks.' Stones from the building were used to make an arbour at Ince Hall (in Ince Green Lane) and the original key is in the possession of Wigan Heritage Services.

In October 1862 a meeting of the Borough Council was held in the Corporation Hall to discuss the building of a new town hall. Several sites were suggested, including behind the smithies in Wallgate (i.e. the site of the present post office), a plot in Millgate, and a piece of land next to Robinson's brewery in Chapel Lane (King Street at this time ended at the junction with Rodney Street, and there was no access to Chapel Lane). This last site was chosen because it was the cheapest and, after purchasing it, the Corporation would be able to extend King Street to Chapel Lane. Borough offices, later used as a town hall, were built on the King Street site in 1866–7.

The building cost £12,000 and the architects were Nuttall and Cook. It lacks the grandeur of many Victorian town halls, but it has some interesting architectural details. In 1890 the room which previously provided accommodation for the Quarter Sessions underwent considerable alterations and was converted into a Council Chamber. The Council Chamber is noted for the large number of coats of arms with which it is decorated, many in stained glass.

In 1990 the premises of the former Wigan College of Technology in Library Street were converted into a new town hall. It was officially opened by the Princess of Wales in 1991.

A painting of the Market Place, showing the Moot Hall as it was before the re-building of 1829.

The only known photograph to show the Moot Hall is this one of the Wallgate entrance to the Market Place. Part of the building, including the colonnade, can be seen on the right.

The Corporation or New Town Hall (1720–1882) in Wigan Market Place.

The Town Hall (built 1866) at the junction of King Street and Rodney Street.

Mrs Julia Walkden was the first woman to stand in a municipal election in Wigan. She was the defeated Labour candidate in a by-election in All Saints Ward in October 1919. She had begun her working life as a domestic servant, but had later gone to work in a cotton mill.

Nurse Hogg became Wigan's first lady councillor in 1920, representing Labour. She began her working life in a cotton mill and trained as a nurse after she married.

Elizabeth McAvoy was Wigan's first Conservative lady councillor. She was elected in 1923.

WIGAN COUNTY BOROUGH
MUNICIPAL ELECTION, 1929.

VOTE FOR MRS. ALSTEAD,
THE PEOPLE'S CANDIDATE.

Mrs Alstead was the Liberal candidate for Swinley Ward in 1929. Her husband was a former mayor of Wigan and MP for Altrincham.

The Revd Sir H.J. Gunning, Bart, was the last lord of the manor of Wigan. He sold the manorial rights to the Corporation in 1860.

Before the rise of the Labour Party the mayoralty was dominated by landed and business interests. Thomas Eckersley (centre) was mayor in 1842 and 1844.

Mill-owner Thomas Taylor was mayor in 1854. He paid for the building of the public library (now the History Shop).

James Smith (mayor in 1889) with some of the seventeenth-century civic regalia, greater and lesser maces and state sword, given to the town by Charles II, and the mayor's staff of office.

# THE GRAMMAR SCHOOLS

During the Middle Ages schools were part of monastic institutions or attached to chantries. The dissolution of these establishments at the Reformation meant that a new educational structure had to be created. This was done by re-establishing former schools and creating new ones through subscription or the commitment of a local benefactor. This was especially so in Lancashire where gifts for educational purposes far exceeded those given for any other charitable purpose. This enthusiasm for education in the county continued until well into the second half of the seventeenth century.

Grammar schools were established to provide (often gratuitously) education in the learned languages, chiefly Latin and Greek, which were spoken by all educated people in Europe, and were a prerequisite for entrance to university. They were financed by endowment and run by trusts. As the years went by these features became disadvantages rather than advantages. Latin and Greek ceased to be the universal languages of the educated. New subjects began to be studied, which were either not taught in the grammar schools, or, if they were, the pupils had to pay for them. Other educational institutions arose in competition to the grammar schools. The landowners, clergymen and businessmen who made up the trusts, impervious to local opinion and outside the control of the national government, neglected their charges. By the middle of the nineteenth century the grammar schools had reached the nadir of their influence. Many of them were to survive, however, by copying the curriculum of the reformed public schools, and acting as feeder schools to the universities at a time when there were far fewer university places available than there are today.

*Foundation dates of some local grammar schools*: 1568: Blackrod; before 1596: Wigan; 1603: Standish; *c*. 1614: Leigh; 1668: Upholland.

## *The Condition of the Endowed Grammar Schools in 1867*

*Aspull School*
The trustees of this school beg to inform the Commissioners that the present school is in a ruinous state and quite unfit for educational purposes, and that they are using all efforts to erect a building more suitable, and have made application to the Committee of Council on Education to help them.

*Leigh Grammar School*
Small as the endowment of this school is, it does good service by maintaining a higher standard of education than the private adventure schools can maintain and there is therefore all the more reason to regret that its trustees take so little interest in it, and that no effort is made to provide proper school rooms and playground.

*Standish Free Grammar School*
Standish is a village on the London and North-Western Railway, about three miles north of Wigan. Some years ago

its so-called grammar school had sunk to the lowest point of wretchedness. The building was ruinous; the headmaster refused to teach anything but Latin and had only half a dozen scholars in all; the usher in his department, which was quite separate from the headmaster's, gave writing and arithmetic to a handful of children; the trustees paid little attention to the place; allowed the master to charge the charity with debts, and to let its property be depreciated through neglect and disrepair. There was indeed little that could be done, since the master was irremovable.

*Wigan Grammar School*
The causes which prevent the grammar school of this town of more than 40,000 people from being better filled and better taught have nothing peculiar about them; they are those which one finds more or less active for evil in all the manufacturing towns. Wigan is a very rough place, with a large population of colliers and poor Irish immigrants, as well as of factory operatives. It is smoky, irregularly built, and altogether unprepossessing, although lying in a country naturally pretty. Hence a master has little prospect of getting boarders, and the richer townspeople prefer to send their sons to schools at a distance. The poorer shopkeepers use the National or British schools, while many persons among the commercial class believe the grammar school to mainly be a place of classical instruction, and hence prefer the private academies of the town. The boys who come are rude in manners, and quite undisciplined in mind. The masters have within the space of two or three years to civilise as well as to teach them, and in this difficult task find no support from the trustees or other persons in the town, who, so far as appears, are, both rich and poor, wholly indifferent to education. These difficulties would not prevent an energetic man who came fresh to the place from improving the character of the school, but they naturally discourage one who has long laboured under their blighting shade, and who has repeatedly seen his own plans for making things better frustrated by the apathy of those to whom he appealed for help.

*Schools Enquiry Commission* (1867–8)

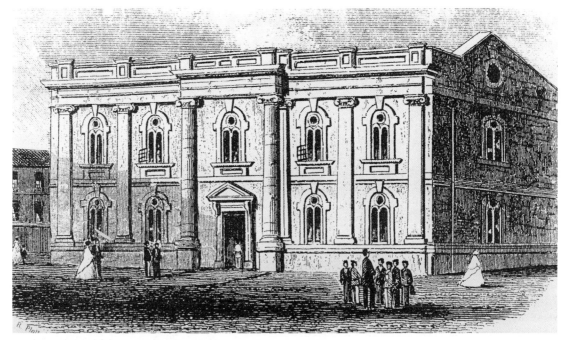

The first purpose-built Wigan Grammar School was situated at the River Douglas end of School Lane. It was demolished in 1723 and the new school shown here was built on the site of what is now the History Shop in Rodney Street.

In 1874 the Rodney Street School was demolished and a public library built on the site. A new school on the Mesnes (shown here) was opened in 1879. Both the library and the school were designed by Alfred Waterhouse RA.

In 1936 Waterhouse's building was demolished, and the much larger school shown here was built on the site. The architect was Alan E. Munby MA, FRIBA.

# WIGAN GIRLS' HIGH SCHOOL

Laying the foundation stone of a new building for the Wigan Girls' High School in March 1915. The building is now Mab's Cross Primary School.

A school group, *c.* 1920.

An art lesson in progress.

In the science
class.

A domestic
science lesson.

'Suspended
animation' in the
gym.

# THE CONSERVATIVES

Conservatism is an attitude of mind that prefers institutions and practices that are manifestations of stability and continuity. As a modern political movement it developed as a reaction to the French Revolution of 1789. Its chief philosophical advocate was Edmund Burke, who argued for government by an ethically trained aristocracy. Locally, its main supporters during this period were Sir Robert Holt Leigh of Hindley Hall, and J. Hodson Kearsley. In the election of April 1831 they failed to prevent the election of a reformer. The Great Reform Act, which did away with the system of rotten boroughs, and extended the franchise, was passed the following year.

Once the Reform Act had been passed Wigan was represented by a succession of Liberal and Conservative MPs until the voters found their spokesman in Sir Francis Sharp Powell, Bt, who represented the town from 1885 to 1910. Like other Conservative MPs for Wigan, he stressed his local connections, and was seen to be generous to the town (he paid for the erection of a children's library, for example). But he also benefited working-class voters in other ways, in his support for factory legislation and improvements in public health, for example. On the other hand he profited from antagonism to Irish immigrants by his opposition to Home Rule for Ireland, and he gained the support of churchgoers by his opposition to local authority schools.

He retired in 1910 because of increasing deafness. A statue of him was placed in Mesnes Park.

Sir Robert Holt Leigh of Hindley Hall.

Sir Francis Sharp Powell, Conservative MP for Wigan from 1885 to 1910.

Campaigning in Upholland for A. Stanley, the son of the sixteenth Earl of Derby, and the Conservative candidate for the Ormskirk constituency in January 1910.

# WORKING MEN!
## Consider the following Facts.
# LORD LINDSAY,

Through the Wigan Coal and Iron Company, pays annually in Wages

# THREE HUNDRED & FORTY THOUSAND POUNDS!
# MR. KNOWLES

### PAYS IN WAGES

## Two Hundred & Thirty Thousand Pounds

### A YEAR!

These large amounts are paid in addition to something like FIFTY-TWO THOUSAND POUNDS for Goods supplied by Tradesmen in the Town.

*They pay in Rates and Taxes* **Twelve Thousand Pounds** *yearly.*

## Total amount paid by Conservative Candidates in the Town

# £634,000

*Six Hundred and Thirty-four Thousand Pounds!*

---

Messrs. LANCASTER & McCORQUODALE do not pay **ONE FARTHING** in the district, either in Wages or Rates, and have not **ONE PENNY** at stake in the neighbourhood.

WHO, then, are most deserving your support?

WHY, # LINDSAY & KNOWLES

Then Vote for them and see that your Friends do the same.

PLATT, PRINTER, WIGAN.

Before 1885 Wigan sent two MPs to parliament. In this poster the two Conservative candidates stress their local connections. They were elected.

# THE LIBERAL AND LABOUR PARTIES

Wigan has not had a Liberal MP since 1874. The franchise was extended in the late nineteenth century, but it was the Tories, with their paternalistic generosity, who captured the Wigan working-class vote. In the elections of 1892 and 1895 the local Liberals put up a working-class candidate but for tactical reasons only. They were out of sympathy with him, and had to be persuaded by Lord Rosebery to re-adopt him at the 1895 election.

In 1900 the Trades Union Congress cooperated with the Independent Labour Party (founded 1893) to establish the Labour Representation Committee, which took the name of the Labour Party in 1906. The antagonistic attitude of the Wigan Liberals to the working-class movement was perhaps the reason why Wigan was one of the first boroughs to set up a local Labour Representation Committee (in 1903). In the election of 1906 Thornley Smith, the president of the local LRC stood as an 'independent labour' candidate on a platform of women's suffrage, old-age pensions, land nationalisation etc., and won 28.7 per cent of the votes. The first official Labour Party candidate was Harry Twist who won the seat in the election of January 1910.

Since 1918 Wigan has returned only Labour MPs, even electing the Labour candidate after the catastrophe of 1931, when the Labour leadership joined with the Conservatives and Liberals, and only fifty-two Labour MPs were returned to the Commons.

The Reform Club, the former Liberal Party headquarters in King Street West.

Henry Twist, Wigan's first Labour MP, elected in 1910. A colliery checkweighman and a Methodist, he was a typical Labour candidate of the period.

## Wigan Constituency Election Results

| 1885 | F.S. Powell (Cons.) | 14.4% majority. |
|---|---|---|
| 1886 | F.S. Powell (Cons.) | 9.6% |
| 1892 | Sir F.S. Powell, Bt (Cons.) | 1.6% |
| 1895 | Sir F.S. Powell, Bt (Cons.) | 12.4% |
| 1900 | Sir F.S. Powell, Bt (Cons.) | 9.4% |
| 1906 | Sir F.S. Powell, Bt (Cons.) | 17.9% |
| 1910 (Jan.) | H. Twist (Lab.) | 5.6% |
| 1910 (Dec.) | R.J.N. Neville (Cons.) | 6.4% |
| 1918 | J.A. Parkinson (Lab.) | 5.0% |
| 1922 | J.A. Parkinson (Lab.) | 13% |
| 1923 | J.A. Parkinson (Lab.) | 15.2% |
| 1924 | J.A. Parkinson (Lab.) | 15.2% |
| 1929 | J.A. Parkinson (Lab.) | 19.8% |
| 1931 | J.A. Parkinson (Lab.) | 2.2% |
| 1935 | J.A. Parkinson (Lab.) | 22.6% |
| 1942 | W. Foster (Lab.) | unopposed |
| 1945 | W. Foster (Lab.) | 36.4% |
| 1948 | R.W. Williams (Lab.) | 23.3% |
| 1950 | R.W. Williams (Lab.) | 32.5% |
| 1951 | R.W. Williams (Lab.) | 33.8% |
| 1955 | R.W. Williams (Lab.) | 32.2% |
| 1958 | E.A. Fitch (Lab.) | 44.5% |
| 1959 | E.A. Fitch (Lab.) | 34.8% |
| 1964 | E.A. Fitch (Lab.) | 41.2% |
| 1966 | E.A. Fitch (Lab.) | 47.8% |
| 1970 | E.A. Fitch (Lab.) | 36.6% |
| 1974 (Feb.) | E.A. Fitch (Lab.) | 42.6% |
| 1974 (Oct.) | E.A. Fitch (Lab.) | 44.8% |
| 1979 | E.A. Fitch (Lab.) | 29.8% |
| 1983 | R. Stott (Lab.) | 31.7% |
| 1987 | R. Stott (Lab.) | 37.1% |
| 1992 | R. Stott (Lab.) | 39.4% |

Campaigning for Labour in the 1920s. J.A. Parkinson, MP for Wigan from 1918 to 1942, is in the centre.

# BIRTHS, MARRIAGES AND DEATHS

Systematic records of births, marriages and deaths first began to be kept in 1538, when Thomas Cromwell, Henry VIII's vice-regent in ecclesiastical matters, ordered that each parish should keep a register of baptisms, marriages and burials. The earliest records were on loose sheets of paper and many have been lost; but in 1597 Queen Elizabeth ordered that the information be kept in parchment books. From 1598 copies of all entries had to be sent to the local bishop. These copies are known as bishops' transcripts, and are useful for checking illegible or missing entries.

The early entries are in Latin. Often baptisms, marriages and burials are intermingled; sometimes one type will begin in the middle of the book; sometimes another type at the back and upside down, so finding a particular entry can be difficult. In 1711, however, proper register books with ruled lines and numbered pages were introduced, and in 1812 specially printed and separate registers for baptisms, marriages and burials appeared. From that date baptismal entries were to include the names, address and occupation of the parents, and burial entries to include the age and address of the deceased.

Civil registration began in 1837, but some records do not provide complete coverage until 1874, when fines were introduced for non-registration.

The dates from which some local registers have survived are as follows: All Saints', Wigan – 1580; St Wilfrid's, Standish – 1560; St Mary's, Leigh – 1560; All Saints', Hindley – 1698; St Thomas', Upholland – 1600; St Aidan's, Billinge – 1696.

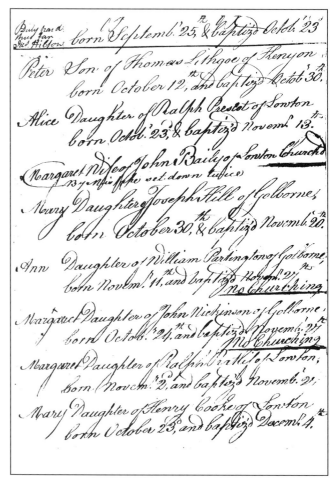

A page from Lowton parish church baptismal register.

## An Unusual Baptism

*All Saints' Church, Wigan*
12th June 1854. John Unknown. The parentage of this child is unknown; he was brought to the workhouse, after having been sold in a public house for three half pence.

This baptismal font was presented to Wigan parish church by Misses Elizabeth and Jane Kenyon of Swinley Hall in 1844.

# Marriage Lines

Some marriage customs are of ancient origin. The bride's veil was supposed to ward off the 'evil eye'. Grains of corn (later rice) were thrown over the couple to ensure fertility. The wedding-cake was originally a loaf made by the bride to show that she was proficient in house-keeping.

In the Middle Ages arranged marriages were the norm, and child betrothals were not uncommon. The marriage ceremony took place in the church porch, and only after the ring had been placed on the bride's finger did the couple enter the church for mass.

In 1603 the Convocation of Canterbury made several regulations, including the necessity of banns or bishop's licence, parent's consent for minors, and closed seasons when marriages were not to take place.

However, marriage by affirmation before witnesses and outside the jurisdiction of the church was still legal. This state of affairs was open to abuse, and in order to curtail the number of clandestine and irregular marriages Hardwicke's Marriage Act of 1753 declared that the ceremony had to be performed by a clergyman of the Church of England in the parish church of one of the parties. Both parties and witnesses were to sign the register.

There was no obligation to record banns until Hardwicke's Act. Licences, issued by the bishop, obviated the need for banns, and were preferred by the upper classes as being more private. Roman Catholics, faced with a law that required them to be married in a church not of their own denomination, sometimes went through a ceremony in both an Anglican and a Roman Catholic Church.

Girls could marry at twelve and boys at fourteen, until 1929, when the lower age limit was raised to sixteen for both.

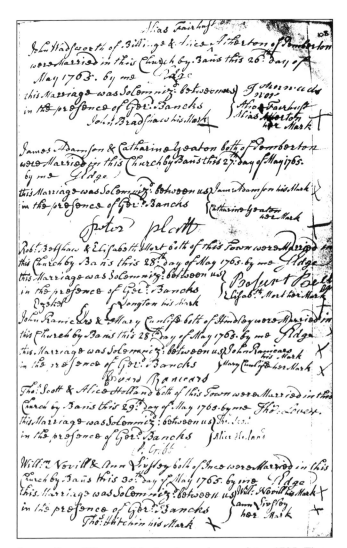

A page from Wigan parish church marriage register, 1705. Those brides and grooms who could not write their names have marked the page with a cross.

A wedding group, 1920s. This decade was the first time in English history that women had worn short skirts, which must have been a shock for the older generation. (J.E. King)

# RECORDING BURIALS

In the early days some clergy only registered burials by Anglican rites, which excluded suicides, excommunicates, executed criminals and unbaptized children. Burials of stillborn children were seldom recorded. Entries were brief, and could be vague; for example: '*All Saints, Wigan*: 14 June 1605 Marie Robinsonne poysoned herselfe; 14 August 1609 The wife of ould blind Bibby; *c.* 15 December 1596 One Fairhurst of Pemberton.'

George Rose's Act of 1812 required burials to be entered in separate books with printed headings. The deceased person's age and address were to be noted, making identification easier.

## Alleged Disrespect to a Funeral at Ince

To the Editor of the *Wigan Observer*:

SIR – Being an attendant at a funeral which took place at the Wigan Cemetery on Saturday last, I wish to call your attention to what I term extraordinary and very unfeeling conduct of the members of a brass band. Whilst the funeral, which consisted of some 80 or 90 persons walking, besides four coaches, holding the deceased and his relatives, was winding its way through Lower Ince, the band was playing, and continued to play, opposite the White Swan Inn, what I consider to be a very lively tune, during the whole of the time the funeral was passing, which caused great indignation amongst onlookers, as well as the funeral party. Whether this unseemly conduct was owing to their ignorance or thoughtlessness, I do not know, but I do sincerely hope that the members of the band in question will give this due consideration, and decide that such an unpleasant incident shall never be repeated. If such a decision is arrived at, they are sure to bestow a favour on many a sorrowing brother and sister, as well as 'One who would do unto others as he would wish to be done by'.

Yours,

B.J.

*Wigan Observer* (22 May 1895)

## Some Unusual Burial Entries

*All Saints', Wigan*

6 July 1612    A bastard of Barlicornes [The mythical John Barleycorn, a familiar figure in old English ballads, was the personification of barley, and the malt liquor made from it, and was associated with debauched living. A child whose father was unknown was attributed to him.]

7 January 1599   Anne, the daughter of Adam Aspull of Hindley, X maid. [i.e. Chrisom maid, a baby girl who died wearing the white chrisom-cloths, which were worn for a month after baptism as a symbol of innocence.]

29 April 1735    Mark Keaton, a soldier shot to death in Wallgate.

15 May 1776    Govan Houston and John Henderson, soldiers of the Scotch Greys burnt to death in the Wallgate.

*Deane (Bolton)*

30 September 1665    John, whose father and mother and place of birth are unknown, commonly called John-of-God's-sending.

*St Wilfrid's, Standish*

24 January 1623    A pore chyld which dyed at Hugh Maudsley his dore in the night. [i.e. a poor child found dead on Hugh Mawdesley's doorstep.]

*St Thomas, Upholland*

12 November 1734    James Stuart, a traveller, who called himself Ye Pretender. [After James Stuart, son of King James II, who was known as the Old Pretender.]

The funeral of one of the Maypole Colliery disaster victims, at Abram, August 1908.

The funeral of an Upholland councillor, 1928. Before the advent of the motor car long lines of mourners would walk with the hearse to the cemetery, and marks of respect for the dead such as the closing of curtains and the removal of hats by bystanders along the route of the procession were assured.

# DISPOSAL OF THE DEAD

The oldest graveyards are oval or circular and are of Celtic origin, rectangular graveyards being introduced during the Anglo-Saxon period. Churchyards are often older than the buildings they contain. Wigan's churchyard was originally oval in shape. The north-east side was narrower than the others, perhaps owing to the proximity of the market-place, and to the fact that there was a practice of burying felons and outcasts on the northern side of graveyards, while the good, honest members of the community were buried on the sunnier east, south and west sides.

The local gentry would have their tombs in special chapels which were part of the church building, while people of the middle ranks of society would be buried under the church floor, as the following entry from the Wigan parish church sexton's daybook shows:

'Isabel, wife of Nicholas Cowell Market place she lies in Bankes' Breadths in the Isle under the flags under that Row towards south Jest at the Heage of the pews. All the pews and Flags fell in When I was Making the Grave that We had all the Flags Both under the pews and in the Isle to New Sett, But when that Grave is opend again you Must tie a Rope Round the one End of the Pew and round the Pillor wich Will Prevent a great Deal of trouble. It will hold 2 More Verry Well.'

Relatives of a deceased person are free to choose any parish they wish for the burial; and everyone has the right of burial in the parish in which he or she died.

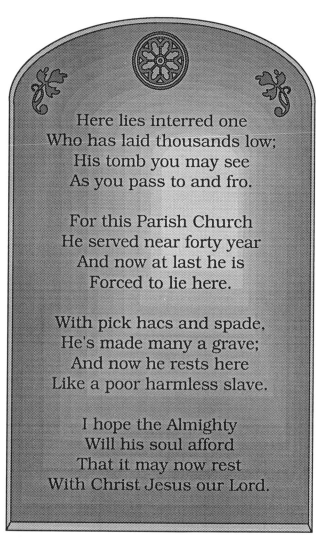

Here lies interred one
Who has laid thousands low;
His tomb you may see
As you pass to and fro.

For this Parish Church
He served near forty year
And now at last he is
Forced to lie here.

With pick hacs and spade,
He's made many a grave;
And now he rests here
Like a poor harmless slave.

I hope the Almighty
Will his soul afford
That it may now rest
With Christ Jesus our Lord.

Epitaph on the tombstone of Andrew Latham, sexton of Wigan parish church, who died in about 1775.

Wigan parish church before the graveyard was extended at the end of the eighteenth century.

# Wigan Parish Church Graveyard

The present state of the graveyard is disgraceful, nor is the rebuilding of the church and the raising of a part of the churchyard a sufficient excuse for the disrespect paid to the remains of the dead and the feelings of the living. During my visit a pile of broken-up coffins stood on one side, and the surface was scattered with bones. It was very evident that much of the disorder was of a permanent character, and due to the want of proper space for burials. The churchyard is surrounded on three sides by a low and dense population. I found a great indisposition to give evidence upon this point, but loud general complaints of the want of a cemetery, in the necessity for which I fully concur.

Clarke, George T., *Report to the General Board of Health . . . into . . . the sanitary conditions of the inhabitants of the Borough of Wigan* (1849)

Wigan Cemetery in Lower Ince was opened in 1856.

# THE VOLUNTEERS

Before 1660 there was no standing army in England. The principal means of defending the country were the county militias, which were raised on the feudal principle of arming each and every able-bodied man. The militia proved to be unreliable compared with the volunteer companies (the first of which was formed in 1537) and were gradually replaced by them.

Several volunteer companies were raised in the Wigan district during the Napoleonic wars and were disbanded afterwards. However, several weeks after the Peterloo Massacre (in 1819) several Wigan gentlemen decided to form a troop of Yeomanry Cavalry. This troop lasted (as part of the Duke of Lancaster's Own Yeomanry Cavalry) until 1880, when it was disbanded. In 1859 Wigan mill-owner N. Eckersley raised the 21st Lancashire Rifle Volunteers, and after several changes of name they became, in 1886, the 1st Volunteer Brigade, the Manchester Regiment. A drill hall was opened for them in Powell Street in 1884. Many saw the active service in the Boer War.

In 1908 Lord Haldane reorganized the country's military forces and created the Territorial Force, which was intended for home defence, while the Regular Army served abroad. On 1 April of that year the Wigan Volunteers became the 5th Battalion, the Manchester Regiment.

On the outbreak of war in August 1914 the Regular Army was moved to the mainland of Europe, and the Territorial Force moved into position to defend the British Isles against invasion. It was not long, however, before the East Lancashire Division, of which the 5th Manchesters formed a part, had left Southampton for Egypt.

Lieutenant-Colonel Richard A. ffarington in the uniform of the Wigan Volunteers.

Men of the Wigan Volunteers in camp, *c.* 1890.

A recruiting poster for the Wigan Volunteers.

Men of the Wigan Territorials in the drill hall at the outbreak of the First World War, August 1914.

# THE FIRST WORLD WAR

The immediate cause of the First World War was the assassination of the Austrian Archduke Franz Ferdinand by a Serb nationalist on 28 June 1914. In retaliation Austria presented Serbia with an ultimatum that she could not accept, and war broke out between the two countries. The chief states of Europe, locked into two rival alliances, became involved, and, as many of them had colonies abroad, the conflict became a world war.

As far as Britain was concerned the main theatre of war was the western front, which lay in France and Belgium. As Britain was not invaded civilians were not directly affected by the conflict, with the exception of those living in towns that were the target of air raids.

Wigan was bombed on 12 April 1918. On that day five Zeppelins left Germany to strike at Britain. One of them was the L61, which flew over Yorkshire and into Cheshire before turning northwards and dropping two bombs on Bold, St Helens. As it approached Wigan the crew saw the glare from the open blast furnaces at the Kirkless ironworks. The blast furnaces were soon shut, and in the darkness the airship dropped seventeen bombs, the first damaging a house in Preston Street, Lower Ince, and the last falling behind the Crown Hotel in New Springs. Five people were killed and nine injured.

The war ended with the signing of the armistice on 11 November 1918. Britain and its allies had lost about 5,000,000 men; Germany and its associates had lost about 3,400,000. The total wounded on both sides was about 21,000,000.

Bernard Wickham, only son of the Revd William Wickham, vicar of St Andrew's, was typical of the young officers who gave their lives for their country during the First World War.

A tram disguised as a tank passes Pemberton Library during Wigan Tank Week, 15–20 April 1918.

The return of the colours of the 5th Battalion, the Manchester Regiment at the end of the First World War.

The unveiling of Wigan's war memorial, 1925.

A sacrifice soon forgotten? Memorials of the First World War are removed from Mesnes Park, having been sold for scrap in June 1935.

# THE SECOND WORLD WAR

The British government began making preparations for civil defence as early as 1935. Observation of the effect of the bombing of civilian targets in China and Spain determined the action taken by the government. Air raid precautions (ARP) included the construction of air raid shelters, both in the town centres, where shop basements were converted into shelters, and in gardens where small corrugated-iron Anderson shelters were erected. Temporary mortuaries, first aid posts and emergency feeding centres were also set up. The auxiliary fire services were extended. The government was particularly concerned about the use of poison gas by the enemy, and everyone was issued with a gas mask. A network of air raid wardens was ready for duty in the event of bombing raids.

Luckily Wigan suffered very little bomb damage. St Paul's Church and St Margaret's Home, Goose Green, were damaged in August 1940, and the Independent Methodist Church in Greenough Street was hit in September of that year.

The government moved sections of the population away from the most obvious target areas. Children from London were evacuated to Wigan, as were people from Liverpool, at the time when that city was suffering a series of bombing raids.

There were other visitors too. French sailors were billeted in Ashton after the fall of France, and later a camp for Italian and German prisoners of war was built near the village. Native soldiers of the (British) Indian Army visited Wigan in October 1943, and American forces had a camp at Burtonwood.

A notice calling on civilians to join the ARP.

These men at New Springs did. With their sandbags, steel helmets, gas masks and rattles, they were ready for anything 'Jerry' could throw at them. (J. Corfield)

Sikh and Gurkha troops of the (British) Indian Army visited Wigan in October 1943.

American troops parade through Wigan at the end of the Second World War.

# LAW AND ORDER

Wigan enjoyed a degree of independence in maintaining law and order with the granting of its first charter in 1246, and only with the creation of a Greater Manchester police force and new magistrates' courts in the 1970s has this been largely dissolved.

By the seventeenth century, when the surviving town records commence, it is clear that most petty offences, criminal and civil, were being tried either in the manorial court leet or the borough courts of pleas or sessions. More serious cases such as murder were heard in the central assize courts, and the county justices met by adjournment at Wigan. The Duchy and Palatine courts of Lancaster exercised their own jurisdiction and cases of immoral behaviour were heard by the bishop of Chester's courts (Wigan being in Chester diocese) or at York.

The average Wigan citizen, therefore, would usually be heard in his own town when it came to cases of theft, assault, debt recovery and disputes with neighbours. In the seventeenth and eighteenth centuries typical punishments were small fines of a few shillings, confinement in the stocks or a whipping at the whipping post in the old market-place, or, for common scolds (invariably women), wearing the bridle or ducking in the cuck stool. Only two presentments for witchcraft have been found in this period. Cases of verbal abuse were common and many people were presented for abusing the mayor or other officials of the town, and these offenders were often punished by being made to apologize or repent in public. The philosophy of punishment was usually to humiliate the offender and make sure his crime was known to everybody; only rarely was imprisonment resorted to.

A notice put out by Lowton farmers, in 1825, stating that stealing from gardens and orchards was now punishable by transportation, and that they would be prosecuting anyone found stealing their fruit.

## A Dispute over Ince Moss

In 1491 a dispute over Ince Moss occurred between Thomas Gerard, Lord of Ince, and his kinsman Sir Thomas Gerard, Lord of Bryn. The following extract is taken from the records of the Duchy Court of Lancaster.

First the said Sir Thomas caused 58 of his servants and tenants the Monday next before the feast of St Martin last past, to come to the said manor of Ince and there with spades and shovels to cast up a ditch in the freehold and several grounds of plaintiff called Ince Moss otherwise Turnesshe Moss, and by force expulsed plaintiff from his old inheritance whereof he and his ancestors have been lawfully seised 'time without mynd'. . . .

After this Sir Thomas Bokeley of Ashton, chaplain to the said Sir Thomas Gerard, James Lawe of the same, yeoman, Humphrey Lawe of the same, yeoman, Thomas Stanley, gentleman, Thomas Hyton, yeoman, William Williamson, yeoman, Lawrens Pendilbury, yeoman, William Leche, yeoman, John Lawe, yeoman, and John Williamson, yeoman, all of the same town, not fearing the King's laws, in a most riotous manner, came to the said moss the 8th March last, and again ditched up the said ditch; they also came to the said manor of Ince, broke plaintiff's closes, and drove away 17 cattle (several of which were milk cattle) and oxen with 1 horse, and unlawfully 'pynned' them at the manor place of the said Sir Thomas called the Bryn, and kept them there three weeks and more, to the great loss of plaintiff and his tenants. . . .

On the 5th April, 6 Henry VII being Shere Thursday the said Sir Thomas with many riotous persons came to the said manor of Ince, bringing with them great mastive dogs 'Grewhondes', and hounds which they set upon the beasts of plaintiff's tenants, 'therwith shouting and horns blowing', and the said dogs 'bott the tayles and eres' of some of the said beasts and drove others into the mire and ditches whereby they were in great danger of being destroyed and lost.

On the 11th April next following the said Sir Thomas sent word to plaintiff that if he dare presume to come to his parish church of Wigan upon the 'other day' he would scour the streets of plaintiff and his company, and upon the said 'other day' which was the 12th day of April, being Thursday in Easter week the said Sir Thomas came to Wigan for that purpose, having with him more than 100 riotous people, and when he saw that the plaintiff was not there he declared openly in the said town that if plaintiff dare come there on the Sunday following being 15th April, that he would put him in jeopardy of his life, but plaintiff having heard of his evil intentions, and in 'eschewying murdre or betyng' of him or his servants has ever since absented himself from his said parish church on Sundays and holy days. . . .

# Extracts from Wigan's Court Records

Michaelmas Leet, 1694. Peter Baldwine presented for saying 'All the Burgesses of Wigan are knaves or most of them Mr Maior [i.e. the Mayor] and all'.

Michaelmas Leet, 1697. John Stables and Anne his wife for calling Jane Faireclough, widow, 'Druncken whore and druncken Bitch', and the said Jane for calling the said John and Anne, 'Druncken Bitch and druncken whore'.

Michaelmas Leet, 1704. Richard Hulme fined for harbouring Richard Lithgoe, husbandman, and for undermining the street in search of coal.

Easter Leet, 1707. Gabriel Wood and Robert son of James Coope for gameing and playing of Tennis Ball on Easter Sunday last upon the Schoole Common.

Wigan Borough Quarter Sessions. William Marsden aged 16 and James Fisher aged 13, Committed 3rd January 1833 by J. Woodcock and J. Lord, Esqs, charged upon oath with having at Wigan feloniously stolen a quantity of Black Puddings, the property of John Cox.

Wigan Borough Quarter Sessions. 10 December 1837. Nathaniel Mason, labourer, William Marsden, labourer and William Drape, labourer, were charged with breaking and entering into the house of Augusta Garnett and stealing 'two hundred and forty pieces of the current copper coin of the Realm called pennies of the value of one Pound and four hundred and eighty pieces of the current copper coin of the Realm called halfpennies of the value of one Pound one silver spoon of the value of one penny and another spoon of the value of one penny and one Drawer of the value of one penny'. Mason was sentenced to 18 months hard labour, Draper to nine months hard labour, and Marsden to be transported for seven years.

# A Strange Case of Manslaughter

A strange case of manslaughter occurred at the Edge Green Colliery, Ashton-in-Makerfield in 1876.

A collier named Henry Birchall went down the pit to remove a windlass which had two legs. He could only get one leg down, and, as the light was poor, he unlocked his lamp and held the naked light to the roof to get a better view and see what was holding the leg. Suddenly there was a small explosion, and a ball of fire appeared. Birchall jumped back, took off his cap, and wafted the ball of fire away. It shot down the workings, becoming larger as it moved, to where two other colliers were working. These poor fellows were burned to death, and Birchall was charged with manslaughter.

Aspull police station. The Wigan Borough Police were founded in 1836, and the Lancashire County Constabulary in 1839. In 1844 there were only three police stations in the district, at Wigan, Pemberton and Leigh.

# PUBS AND BREWING

Brewing was probably introduced into Britain during the Neolithic period, at the same time as barley, with which it is closely connected. Until the Middle Ages brewing was mainly carried out at home by the women of the household. Some women, known as 'ale-wives', began to sell ale to travellers and other customers. People began to stay in these houses to consume the drink they bought, and to enjoy the company of other drinkers, and our present pubs developed from these houses. Ale was brewed without the use of hops. Beer, made with hops, was introduced to England in the early fifteenth century.

The first surviving list of ale-house keepers in Wigan (the houses are not named) dates from 1635. There are about fifty names on the list, to serve a population of about three thousand.

The authorities seem to have periodically considered the number of retail outlets selling alcoholic drinks to be excessive. The Licensing Statute of 1495 gave Justices of the Peace power to supervise and suppress local ale sellers, and other controlling acts followed. Locally, Edward Fleetwood (Rector of Wigan from 1571 to 1604) attempted to limit the sale of ale by forbidding less than a quart to be sold to any one customer at a time (an innovation that could have had the opposite effect from that intended!). In 1890, as a preliminary to reducing the number of outlets, a survey of public houses was conducted in Lancashire to determine the accommodation they provided and the distances between them. Some of the results are published here.

A rural off-licence at Little Scotland, Blackrod.

## *Some Local Pubs in 1890*

| Name and situation | Accommodation | Stabling | Distance from two nearest adjoining public houses |
|---|---|---|---|
| Hare and Hounds Church Lane, Lowton | 1 bed, can feed 3 persons | for 3 horses | 50yd/1½ miles |
| Ram's Head Slag Lane, Lowton | 1 bed, can feed 2 persons | for 4 horses | 50yd/1½ miles |
| Stork Inn Chapel Brow, Billinge | 5 beds, can feed 100 persons | for 30 horses | 55yd/800 yd |
| Ben Johnson Park Lane, Pemberton | No beds, can feed 5 persons | for 4 horses | 733yd/880yd |
| Bold Hotel Worsley Mesnes, Pemberton | No beds, can feed 10 persons | for 2 horses | 183yd/1,286yd |
| Tippings Arms Worsley Mesnes, Pemberton | 2 beds, can feed 15 persons | for 2 horses | 183yd/1,469yd |
| Belle Vue Inn Belle Green Lane, Ince | 2 beds, can feed 6 persons | none | 100yd/400yd |
| Manley Hotel Ince Green Lane, Ince | 1 bed, can feed 4 persons | for 3 horses | 300yd/300yd |

*County Palatine of Lancaster: Return of Public Houses and Beerhouses (1890)*

# The Colliers and Drink

Is it considered discreditable for a man to be seen drunk? – No it is considered no disgrace to be seen drunk and disorderly; every pay night they come to town, and they are drunk and disorderly upon these occasions; their wives usually accompany them, and leave the children to fend for themselves.

In visiting the houses of the colliers, are scenes of riot and debauchery frequent? – In visiting two houses lately, a policeman reported that he saw the wife on the floor in a state of beastly intoxication, and the children half-naked, sitting on their heels around the fire. . . .

Have you much difficulty in clearing the public houses of the colliers on Saturday nights? – Yes, we have; we go round at 12 o'clock, and it is generally between one and two before we can get them cleared out, and when they go home they are noisy and quarrelsome in the street. The White Lion was fined yesterday for having between 30 and 40 people in the house at one o'clock on Sunday morning the 2nd of May – most of the 40 were colliers. The Crofter's Arms, the Windsor Castles in the Scholes, and several others, are great houses of resort for colliers.

What are the pursuits on Sundays? – It is a custom of the colliers on a Sunday to have a gallon or two gallon bottle of beer and take it to their own houses, or bask in the fields if there is sunshine, and sometimes they will sit on the pit-bank and drink it.

Mr Latham, Chief Constable of Wigan, in evidence to the Children's Employment Commissioners (1841)

(It should be added that the police were not entirely innocent. The proprietors of the Wigan Brewery complained to the Watch Committee that policemen were found drinking in the brewery's store-rooms and several officers were dismissed for drunkenness.)

Drinkers at Bottling Wood in the early years of the twentieth century.

# DO YOU REMEMBER THESE PUBS?

The Dog i' th' Thatch, Standishgate.

The Ropemakers Arms, Caroline Street.

The Harrogate Inn, Harrogate Street.

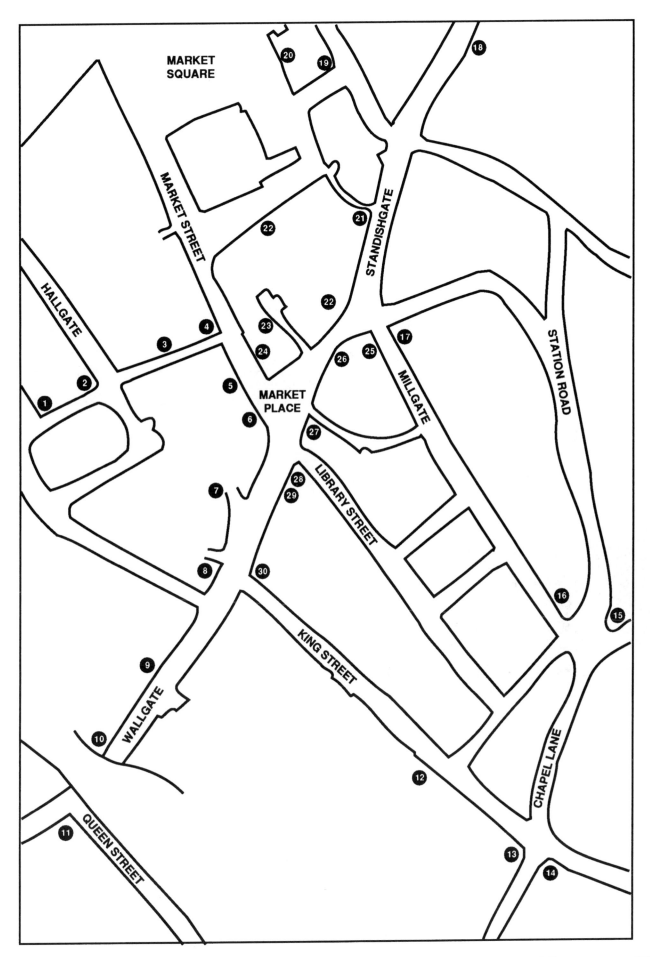

Numbered on the map are Wigan's town centre pubs as they were about forty years ago. How many can you name? (Answers on page 158)

# LOCAL BREWERIES

## Some Oldfield Brewery Public Houses

Bankes' Arms, Wallgate
Ben Jonson, Warrington Road
Black Bull, Hardybutts
Black Swan, Scholes
Bluebell, Scholes
Bold Hotel, Worsley Mesnes
Bricklayers Arms, Hallgate
Cotton Tree Inn, Hardybutts
Enfield Inn, Enfield Street
Foundry Inn, Warrington Lane
Griffin Hotel, Standishgate
Saracens Head, Wigan Lane
Ropemakers Arms, Caroline Street

## Some Sumners (Haigh) Public Houses

Hare and Hounds, Aspull
Running Horses, Aspull
Balcarres Arms, Haigh
Crawford Arms, Red Rock
Hand and Heart, Market Street, Hindley
Spinners' Arms, Castle Hill Road
Conquering Hero, Ince
Rifleman Inn, Caroline Street, Ince
Plough and Harrow, Shevington
Bay Horse, Whelley
Dog and Partridge, Chapel Street, Pemberton
Crown Inn, Platt Lane

A vestige of the Oldfield Brewery Company on a former pub in Wigan Market Place. Founded in 1876, the company was taken over by Walker Cain in 1926. The brewery was in Poolstock Lane.

Airey's Victoria Brewery, Westwood Road, off Poolstock Lane. Founded in 1906, it was taken over by Walker Cain in 1926. (G. Hamer)

140

John Sumner and Company Ltd were taken over by Greenhall Whitley in 1931.

Workers at Haigh Brewery.

Haigh windpump was erected in about 1845 to deliver water from two ponds to the reservoir at Haigh Brewery, the chimney of which can be seen in the background.

# THE PLEASURES OF THE CHASE

During the Middle Ages much of what is now Lancashire was royal forest, in which hunting rights were reserved for the king. The manorial lords had their parks. These were enclosures in which game such as boar and wild cattle, but especially deer, were kept and hunted as occasion required. The method used was to drive a selected animal to a stand from which it was shot by the lord with a crossbow. The location of such parks can sometimes be determined by place-names. Park House Farm and Park Lane Farm point to the former park of the Gerards of Bryn Hall.

The process of disafforestation gave the gentry the freedom to hunt with hounds across country. By the late eighteenth century fox hunting was replacing deer and hare hunting in popularity.

However, in 1850 Major F. Gerard established the Aspull Harriers (hounds used for hunting hares). When he died in 1883 the Hon. W. Gerard (afterwards Lord Gerard) took over. In 1906 the pack consisted of twenty-five couple which hunted a country about 17 miles by 12, consisting chiefly of pasture. A contemporary described the country as 'a very nice one to ride, with plenty of flying fences; it carries a good scent, and sport is excellent'.

## Narrow Escape of a Gentleman While Hunting

On Saturday last, Mr Edward Kearsley, of the Height, near Bolton, was hunting with the Aspull harriers, in Standish, that gentleman having occasion to jump some rails on the bank of a colliery railway, when his horse's hind legs went through some old rotten timber, grown over with grass, which covered the mouth of an old colliery shaft. For a few seconds the horse struggled desperately to obtain a firm footing but was unable to do so, and at last a portion of the surface embankment giving way, he fell backwards to the bottom of the pit, and was killed on the spot. Most miraculously, Mr Kearsley himself escaped. He managed to alight from his horse over his hind-quarters, and succeeded in obtaining a solid footing an instant before the horse fell and was dashed to pieces. It happened that there was nothing whatever, to denote that there was a pit of any description there.

*Wigan Examiner* (29 October 1858)

Major F. Gerard, master of the Aspull Harriers, lived at Aspull House, which stood opposite St Elizabeth's Church.

# ASPULL & CROSTON HUNT STEEPLE CHASES

## MARCH 31st, 1859.

### STEWARDS.

LORD SKELMERSDALE.   SIR ROBERT GERARD.   SIR THOMAS HESKETH.
MAJOR BLUNDELL.      FRED. S. GERARD, Esq.   R. D'TRAFFORD, Esq.
CAPTAIN ANDERTON.   CAPTAIN STARKIE.

FRED. S. GERARD, Esq., Judge.   FRANCIS TWINING, Esq., Treasurer and Secretary.

### First Race, to start at Two o'Clock.

THE PARBOLD STAKES of 3 sovs. each, 2 ft., with a handsome piece of plate added.
—4-year old, 11 st.; five, 12 st. 3 lb ; six and aged, 13 st.   Thoroughbreds to carry 9 lb. extra,
and the winner of any public or private Race or Steeple-chase (matches excepted) 7lb. extra;
of two or more, 14 lb. extra; second horse to save his stake, and the winner to pay 5 sovs.
towards the expenses.

1 Sir Thomas Hesketh's b. h. Billy, aged, h. b.......
2 Mr. Twining ns. bl. m. Peeress, aged, h. b. ........ *Violet and Straw.*
3 Mr. Richardo ns. g. g. The Doctor, aged, h. b. .... *White.*
4 Captain G. N. Starkie's Sepoy, 6 years ...........
5 Mr. M'Culloch's bn. m. Lady Eleanor, aged, h. b... *Blue, B. & W. Cap.*
6 Mr. Edwards ns. g. g. Bobbin-around, aged, h. b. .. *Orange.*
7 Captain Anderton's g. g Balaklava, aged, h. b. .... *Black and White Stripe.*
8 Mr Hills bn. m. Lightheart, aged, h. b. .......... *Orange, Black Hoop and Cap.*
9 Mr. Golding ns. b. m. Creeping Jenny, aged, h. b.. *Blue & White Stripe & W. Cap.*
10 Mr. Twining ns. b. m. Sunset, aged, h. b............ *Scarlet and Black Cap.*

### Second Race, to start at a Quarter to Three o'Clock.

THE CROSTON SELLING STAKES of 20 sovs., added to a Sweepstakes of 2
sovs. each.   The weights and penalties as in the First Race.   The winner to be sold for 80
sovs.; if entered to be sold for 60 sovs. allowed 7lb., for 40 sovs. 14lb., for 25 sovs. 21 lb., and
for 15 sovs. 28lb.   The winner to be sold by Auction immediately after the race, and the
surplus (if any) to go the Race-fund.   The second horse to save his stake, and the winner to
pay 3 sovs. towards the expenses.

1 Mr. Cox's bl. h. Midnight, aged, h. b., £15........ *Violet and Straw Cap.*
2 Mr. Golding ns. c. h. The Baron, aged, h b , £15.. *Blue & White Stripe & Bk. Cap.*
3 Mr. J. Wright's c. m. Misletoe, 6 yrs., h. b., £15.... *Blue and Black Cap*
4 Mr. Hill ns. c. h. First Flight, aged, h. b. £15 ..... *Orange, Bk. Hoop, & O. & B. Cap*

### Third Race, to start at Half-past Three o'Clock.

THE ASPULL HANDICAP of 2 sovs. each, with a handsome piece of plate added;
second horse to save his stake, and the winner to pay 4 sovs. towards the expenses.

1 13st 0lb Mr. Edwards ns. g. g. Bobbin-around,
     aged, h. b. ..................... *Orange*
2 12st 10lb Mr. M'Culloch's bn. m. Lady Eleanor,
     aged, h. b. ..................... *Blue & B. & W. Cap.*
3 12st 8lb Mr. Twining ns b. m. Sunrise, h. b. .. *Scarlet and B. Cap.*
4 12st 8lb Mr. Rawcliffe ns Starlight, aged, h.b... *Violet and Straw cap.*
5 11st 10lb Mr. M'Culloch's b.m. Alma, aged, h b... *Blue & B Cap.*
6 11st 7lb Mr. Golding ns b m Creeping Jenny, h b.. *Blue & White stripe & W. Cap.*
7 10st 8lb Mr. Hill's b. m Dairy Maid, h. b....... *Orange and Black Hoop and Cap.*

# ASSORTED SPORTS

Miners about to go shooting and fishing on one of Wigan's flashes.

A wrestling match at Aspull, 1920s.

Spring View ladies' football team.

Wigan had a very strong water polo team in the first quarter of the twentieth century. (M.F. Lupton)

Studying the form at Poolstock dog track, 1950s.

## The Disgraceful Custom of Racing Naked

Yesterday (Friday) at the Wigan County Police Court, Before Messrs Thomas Marshall and James Taylor, Joseph Barker, John Wadsworth, Robert Heyes, John Lowe, Wm. Pennington, Harry Green, and Thomas Littler, all young men, were charged with riotous and disorderly at Billinge-Chapel-End, on Monday last. – Two constables stated that the defendants were swearing and gambling on Monday at Billinge-Chapel-End, with about one hundred others, all of whom were on the highway. Two of the defendants – Barker and Little – were racing, and the betting was as to who would win. Both the runners were stripped entirely of their clothing. – Superintendent Clarkson said it was quite a practice at Billinge Chapel End for youths and young men to run naked, and ladies and ministers of religion had written to the head office at Preston complaining of it. They had done all they possibly could to put it down. – The magistrates bound Littler and Barker over to keep the peace for six months in two sureties of £5 each; the charge against Heyes was dismissed, and the remainder had to pay costs.

*Wigan Examiner* (30 November 1878)

John Harland in his *Lancashire Legends* (1873) wrote: 'Races by nude men are not yet extinct in many parts of Lancashire, notwithstanding the vigilance of the county police.'

# THE SILVER SCREEN

The following cinemas were operating in Wigan in 1952:
Carlton Cinema, Ormskirk Road, Pemberton
County Playhouse, King Street
Court Cinema, King Street
Empire Cinema, Market Place
Gidlow Picture House, Gidlow Lane
Palace Cinema, King Street
Pavilion Cinema, Library Street
Prince's Cinema, Wallgate
Queen's Cinema, Ormskirk Road, Pemberton
Ritz Cinema, Station Road
Scholes Picture House, Scholes
Labour Hall Cinema, Scholes

SOME FACTS ABOUT LOCAL CINEMAS:
Buddy Holly played at the ABC (Ritz) on 18 March 1958.
Prince's Cinema opened as the King's Electric Theatre in 1911. This was the first purpose-built cinema in Wigan. It was rebuilt in 1934. Other buildings which regularly showed films in the early years were the Queen's Hall Methodist Mission, The Empire Music Hall, and the Alliance Hall (now Wigan Little Theatre).
The last film to be shown at the Court Cinema was *The Sound of Music*.

*DO YOU KNOW?*
Which sport was played in the Pavilion before it was converted into a cinema? (Answer on page 158)

A notice for the last film shown at the Labour Hall Cinema, Scholes. The cinema closed in 1955.

Staff of the Scholes Picture House. This cinema closed in 1959 and was demolished in October 1960.

The Pavilion, situated at the bottom of Library Street, began showing films in 1910. It was demolished in 1959 to make way for the new swimming baths.

The Royal Court in King Street followed the classic pattern of conversion from a theatre to a cinema, and from a cinema to a bingo club.

The Ritz opened in March 1938. The first film shown was *Lost Horizon* with Ronald Colman and Jane Wyatt.

# THE ENTERTAINERS

Over the years, Wigan has been able to boast of a large number of stars who have been associated with the area. Some were born here, while others moved into the area to live for a short period. If one asks people to name a personality associated with Wigan, the name that generally springs to mind is that of George Formby. Unfortunately, his fame has tended to overshadow the many other personalities of both stage and screen. However, this should not detract from Formby's successful stage and film career which endeared him to his adoring public.

The illustrations chosen are intended to show some of the other local personalities who have made names for themselves in the wider world outside the area.

Besides the personalities illustrated on these two pages others who haven't been included are Margery Booth, the Wigan-born contralto who became a British Secret Service agent while remaining an opera singer in Nazi Germany; Roy Kinnear, the popular comedy actor who died in 1988 while filming in Toledo, Spain; Sir Ian McKellen, the famous Shakespearean actor who lived in Parsons Walk and attended Wigan Grammar School; Rosalind Plowright, the noted soprano who attended Notre Dame High School; Frank Randle (real name Arthur McEvoy), who became a manic Lancashire comedian; Ted Ray (Charlie Olden), the Wigan-born comedian who appeared in numerous films but who shot to fame with his radio programme *Ray's a Laugh*; and finally Dame Eva Turner, the Oldham-born soprano whose father was a native of Standish.

These are only a few of the stars who may be recalled by an older generation. The list is probably a good deal longer, so apologies have to be made for not including everyone by name.

Marie Ault once held the record for the largest number of different parts played by an actor or actress. Here she is seen as Mrs Jilke in the film *Love on the Dole*.

Eleanor Robson was born in Wigan, but emigrated to the USA at an early age. She became an internationally famous actress, returning to Britain for her London stage debut in 1904.

Colin Bean achieved national recognition through his portrayal of Private Sponge in the television comedy series *Dad's Army*.

Beth Ellis was a writer, some of whose books, such as *Barbara Winslow, Rebel*, were adapted for the stage and the cinema.

Lily Brayton was born in Hindley. She became a well-known actress on the London and provincial stage. This photograph dates from 1908, and shows her in *The Two Pins*, a comedy set in the Middle Ages.

George Formby jnr was the son of a famous music hall comedian. He established himself on the provincial stage before beginning a recording and film career which made him a household name.

# WIGAN RUGBY CLUB

The English Rugby Union was the original controlling body for all the country's rugby football clubs, so it was under their aegis that the game first existed in Wigan. It was members of the Wigan Cricket Club, established in 1848, who decided they would try rugby and thus extend their sporting activities through the winter months. Properly organized sports activities in those days were the preserve of the professional classes, and the Wigan Rugby Football Club, formed in 1872, was no exception; for example, the three Walker brothers of the local engineering firm (see page 72) were all involved in the early days of the club.

After a period of initial enthusiasm things went off the boil and only amalgamation with the Upholland Club kept rugby going in the town at one stage. Ground availability was another problem in the early days as pitches tended to be acquired by developers as the population, housing requirements and industry all expanded rapidly.

By the mid-1880s the team was once more on the ascendancy, becoming one of the leading clubs in the north of England. Competition was rife, and despite being an amateur game a trend developed of the bigger clubs managing to persuade star players from smaller clubs to change allegiance.

Working-class men whose initial contact with the game was merely as spectators gradually became more involved in playing, but the six day working week was then the norm and for many playing rugby on a Saturday afternoon meant a loss in wages. The north of England clubs in particular lobbied the ruling body to allow compensation payments, but the English Rugby Union hierarchy were not to be moved from the principle of total amateurism, and started to impose fines on clubs who were allegedly offering inducements to players. Matters came to a head in 1894 when Wigan, Leigh and Salford were all suspended. The outcome was that a significant number of prominent northern clubs, including Wigan, resigned from the English Rugby Union and ran their own competition administered by a new body initially called the Northern Rugby Football Union, but in 1922 renamed the Rugby Football League.

At the time of the formation of the Northern Union, Wigan played at the Prescott Street cricket ground, but had to look elsewhere when it was sold in 1901. The 1901/2 season home matches were played at Springfield Park, where the rugby men shared the facilities with a soccer club called Wigan United. The rugby club didn't like the joint use so obtained some meadowland alongside the River Douglas close to the town centre, and so was created their famous Central Park ground. The first match there on Saturday 6 September 1902 resulted in a 14 to 8 points victory over Batley.

At the end of the 1908/9 season, Wigan gained their first Championship win and in the summer of 1910 contributed five players to the Great Britain squad in the code's first ever tour of Australia.

Many talented rugby union players were attracted to the Northern Union game due to the financial rewards, and this was especially the case with the predominantly working class players of the south Wales valleys clubs. Wigan had its fair share of Welsh 'imports', including Cardiff's Jim Sullivan, who was signed in 1921 and continued as a player until February 1946, making some 928 appearances at first class level, 774 of them for Wigan. He was a club captain and fullback of great ability but his supreme talent was in the art of goal kicking, with a career total of 2,867 successful attempts.

The end of the 1928/9 season saw Wigan in a Challenge Cup final with Dewsbury as opponents. What made this fixture extra special was that it was the first final to be played at Wembley Stadium, and Wigan duly took the honours 13 to 2 points.

After a curtailed programme of Second World War fixtures, the club was soon picking up the major trophies in front of huge early post-war crowds. In 1950 the club gained their seventh Championship despite having eight players unavailable, owing to international duty, for the play-off final.

In March 1953 Wigan gained the signature of another young Welshman. This was Billy Boston, who continued as a Central Park favourite for fifteen years.

The fixtures which Wigan rugby fans traditionally look forward to more than any other are the home and away clashes with St Helens and it was such a match, played at Central Park on Good Friday 27 March 1959, that created the ground's record attendance of 47,747.

The 1970s was not a good decade for the Wigan club but the '80s saw the club on the road to recovery and in May 1985 the Challenge Cup was once more in the trophy cabinet after a twenty year absence. Three years later it was back in the cabinet where it was to remain for a remarkable eight seasons.

Wigan rugby's first superstar, Jim Slevin, was one of the first playing members after the club was formed. He went on to play for over twenty years, scoring many spectacular tries, and proving to be a great crowd favourite.

A goal-kicking winger signed from Lancaster in 1903, the elegant Jimmy Leytham became one of the great personalities of the Edwardian era. When he retired in 1912, Leytham had scored more tries (312) than any other player in history.

Players and officials pose with their haul of trophies at the conclusion of the 1908/9 season, the highlight of which was the Club's first ever Championship win. In addition they won the Lancashire Cup, the Lancashire League and the West Lancashire Cup.

An aerial view of Central Park, 1938. In the lower part of the picture can be seen the back of the original Douglas stand. The opposite or 'Popular' side was partially covered by the 'dutch barn' stand erected in 1911/12 and replaced in 1954.

The first tour of Australasia by a Great Britain Northern Union (Rugby League) side took place in 1910 and these five Wigan players were included in the squad. They are: top left, Bert Jenkins; bottom left, Jim Sharrock; centre, Johnny Thomas; top right, Jimmy Leytham; and bottom right, Richard Ramsdale.

151

Joe Egan, reckoned to be one of the finest hookers in history, played at a time when games often contained seventy or eighty scrums. Egan left Wigan to become player-coach at Leigh in 1950 for a then RL record fee of £5,000.

Jim Sullivan made more appearances (928) and kicked more goals (2,867) than any other rugby league player, in a career which spanned twenty-five years. His Wigan career tally of 774 games, 2,317 goals and 4,883 points look likely to stay for ever as club records.

Wigan favourite Billy Boston seen scoring his record-making seventh try in a match against Dewsbury at Central Park on 20 August 1955. On 30 April 1962 he again achieved seven tries in a game, this time away from home against Salford.

One of the game's greatest scrum halves, Andy Gregory, joined his hometown club for a RL record transfer fee of £130,000 from Warrington. He became one of the most decorated players in history before embarking on a coaching career at Salford.

Central Park action during a Challenge Cup second round tie against Halifax on 22 February 1930. Halifax's Mitchell Smith with the ball (left) is tackled by Wigan's New Zealand import Lou Brown. Wigan won the match by 14 points to 5.

Action from the first ever rugby league match to take place at Wembley Stadium. The fixture was the 1928/9 season Challenge Cup Final between Wigan (striped jerseys) and Dewsbury, which Wigan won by 13 points to 2.

The Wigan side of the 1990/1 season with Australian coach John Monie (centre front row). At the time of publication in 1996 nearly all these players had moved to other clubs, retired, or taken up coaching positions, indicating the high player turnover rate in the modern contract orientated game.

# THE POWER OF THE PEN

Wigan and its immediate surroundings have produced a number of significant writers and provided other writers with material.

The writings of Gerrard Winstanley (1609–?) are of world importance in that they are the first detailed expression of the socialist and materialist thought that was to play such a significant role in later centuries. A political activist as well as a writer, the commune he and his followers established was destroyed by the authorities.

One of the most interesting literary figures in the Wigan area was Ellen Weeton (1776–1849), a woman of determination whose misfortunes, including a disastrous marriage and enforced separation from her daughter, are recorded in her journal and letter-books.

The Victorian period produced several writers. Among them were John Critchley Prince (1808–66), who lived in poverty and yet attained immense popularity as a poet, and John Roby (1793–1850) of Haigh, whose fame rests largely on his *Traditions of Lancashire*, written in the style of Sir Walter Scott. J. Monk Foster (1857–1930) worked in the collieries as a child but grew up to become a popular novelist and journalist, even editing his own lively but short-lived newspaper, *The Comet*.

---

*DO YOU KNOW?*

Who, referring to himself, wrote: 'He liked Wigan very much – the people, not the scenery'? (Answer on page 158)

---

## *Gerrard Winstanley puts pen to paper for the last time:*

Here is the righteous law; man, wilt thou it maintain?
It may be, is, hath still, in the world been slain.
Truth appears in light, falsehood rules in power;
To see these things to be, is cause of grief each hour.
Knowledge, why did'st thou come, to wound and not to cure?
I sent not for thee, thou didst me inlure.
Where knowledge does increase, there sorrows multiply,
To see the great deceit, which in the world doth lie:
Man saying one thing now; unsaying it anon,
Breaking all's engagements, when deeds for him are done.
O power where art thou, that must mend things amiss?
Come, change the heart of man, and make him truth to kiss.
O death, where art thou? Wilt thou not tidings send?
I fear thee not; thou are my loving friend.
Come, take this body, and scatter it in the four,
That I may dwell in one, and rest in peace once more.

---

In modern times writers associated with the district have included Kathleen Fidler (1899–1980), a popular writer of children's fiction; John Farrimond of Hindley, a miner who turned to writing novels about colliers and northern life, and Louis Hodgkiss, who turned novelist while unemployed.

Mention Wigan and literature, and most people will think of George Orwell's *The Road to Wigan Pier*, a lively mix of reportage, socialist polemic and idiosyncratic comment.

A recently published novel set in nineteenth-century Wigan is Martin Cruz Smith's *Rose*.

---

February 2d [1824] I have long contemplated writing a History of my life, and yet have deferred it from month to month, from what must appear a very strange reason by any one who sees the quantity of my writings – the reluctance I feel to attempt writing. Whether it proceeds from indolence, or some other undefinable motive, I cannot say; but whether I have a letter to write, a journal, or an account, it seems a task to me; and yet the activity of my mind perpetually urges to me to it. It is a strange contradiction! but are we not all strange contradictory beings.

This day I arranged all my books and writing materials on my table, determining to begin, when such a depression of spirits seized me at the melancholy retrospect, that I could not commence. I wept, I trembled, and my soul utterly refused comfort; like Rachel, I wept for my child. I tried to pray, to sing a hymn, but could do neither. I passed the whole of the day in melancholy inaction; the next day the same. I attempted to sew, I put it away again; I took my flageolet, but it pleased me not, my mind was not in tune; and, living by myself, I had not a human being to speak to. If I had, it would often make me more cheerful, and would help greatly to restore my composure when my spirit is cast down.

12th. I think of my Mary from day to day, and mean immediately to make another attempt to see her, let Mr Grundy treat me as he may. I think he means well upon the whole, but Mr Stock has taken so much pains to prejudice his mind against me, that he is influenced to obey Mr S's tyrannical directions much more decidedly than he ought to be if he were really a Christian; which I hope he is, almost.

*Diary of Ellen Weeton*

---

John Roby, son of a Haigh schoolmaster, wrote music, periodical articles and short stories. He was drowned at sea in 1850.

## John Critchley Prince writes on the death of his infant son:

A dreamy stillness in the calm air slept;
The moon was cloudless, and serenly wept
Her tears of radiance in my lonely room,
Giving a silvery softness to the gloom;
When Death – that mighty and mysterious shade –
Beneath my roof his first dread visit paid, –
His shadowy banner o'er my hearth unfurled,
And broke the spell that bound me to the world.
Oh, mournful task! at that subduing hour
I watched the withering of a cherished flower;
I bent in silence o'er a dying child,
And felt that grief which cannot be beguiled;
Held on my trembling knee his wasted frame,
As the last shadow o'er his features came;
Saw the dull film that veiled his lovely eyes, –
Received upon my lips his latest sighs;
And as the spirit calmly, softly passed,
I knew that I was desolate at last!
A few brief hours and he was borne away,
And laid, soft, sleeping, on his couch of clay.
Fond hearts that loved, and lips that blessed were there,
That swelled with grief, and breathed the parting prayer.
The pastor gave his treasure unto God; –
I only heard the booming of the clod
That closed for ever on my darling son,
And told that love's last obsequies were done;
Then looking, lingering still – I turned again
To quell my grief amid the haunts of men.

*from A Father's Lament*

John Critchley Prince was born in Wigan in 1808, and died in Hyde in 1866. He was the author of five volumes of poems.

It is not long since conditions in the mines were worse than they are now. There are still living a few very old women who in their youth have worked underground, with a harness round their waists and a chain that passed between their legs, crawling on all fours and dragging tubs of coal. They used to go on doing this even if they were pregnant. And even now, if coal could not be produced without pregnant women dragging it to and fro, I fancy we should let them do it rather than deprive ourselves of coal. But most of the time, of course, we should prefer to forget that they were doing it. It is so with all types of manual work; it keeps us alive, and we are oblivious of its existence. More than anyone else, perhaps, the miner can stand as the type of manual worker, not only because his work is so exaggeratedly awful, but also because it is so vitally necessary and yet so remote from our experience, so invisible, as it were, that we are capable of forgetting it as we forget the blood in our veins. In a way it is even humiliating to watch coal-miners working. It raises in you a momentary doubt about your own status as an 'intellectual' and a superior person generally. For it is brought home to you, at least while you are watching, that it is only because miners sweat their guts out that superior persons can remain superior. You and I and the editor of the Times Lit. Supp., and the Nancy poets and the Archbishop of Canterbury and Comrade X, author of 'Marxism for Infants' – all of us really owe the comparative decency of our lives to poor drudges underground, blackened to the eyes, with their throats full of coal dust, driving their shovels forward with arms and belly muscles of steel.

George Orwell, *The Road to Wigan Pier* (1937)

# THE WAY IT MIGHT HAVE BEEN

The historical development of any settlement depends upon many factors. Geology, topography, climate, location, the policies of local and national government, and decisions made by influential individuals, all play their part. Change these ever so slightly, and the history of the settlement is changed into something completely different.

So let's take a peep into some old records and see what might have been for Wigan:

The *Colliery Guardian* of 1 July 1892 stated: 'Petroleum has been found in Great Britain at Worsley, at Wigan, and at Westleigh in the Lancashire coalfield . . . but never in such quantities or under such conditions as to induce the discoverers to work it.'

In the 1920s the Westwood Car Company of Lower Ince was producing a modest range of motor cars. The firm had a good reputation, but it was too small to compete with emerging giants such as Austin and Morris, and production only lasted for six years.

In 1932 Wigan Chamber of Commerce was publicizing a new industry that had been established in the town – the manufacture of 'bijou billiards tables for small houses'. In the same year there was talk of establishing an international airport outside the town. A few years later Wigan's Town Clerk persuaded Air Vice Marshall Longcroft to visit the town with a view to establishing an 'aircraft factory', but the Air Ministry decided that Wigan wasn't a suitable location.

So there we have it. Had things been a little different Wigan would have been at the heart of a major oilfield, served by an international airport, and its chief industries the manufacture of cars and aircraft . . . and, of course, pool tables.

# Wigan As an Air Centre

Will Wigan become a commercial air route centre in the near future?

The Hon. Mrs Victor Bruce, the famous airwoman, paid a secret visit to the town today to discover whether the Town Council would grant her facilities to assist in developing Wigan into an airport from which long-distance flights could be made.

The airwoman, who is on a lecture tour of the North of England, arrived by car from Blackpool, and saw the Mayor (Councillor W.A. Hipwood) to whom she explained her scheme.

With the Mayor's secretary (Mr Wills) she later toured the outskirts of the town, and viewed certain sites at Boar's Head, Standish Woods, and Pemberton, which in the past have been used as landing grounds. I understand that Mrs Bruce favoured the Pemberton site as a likely spot for establishing an air station.

'I understood from what Mrs Bruce told me that her idea is in part to establish an air trading centre here,' the Mayor told me later. . . . 'The scheme seems a sound one, but, of course, the matter, so far as the town itself is concerned, would have to be seriously considered before anything definite could be arranged. . . . '

If Mrs Bruce's scheme is welcomed by the Corporation it is her intention, I believe, to name her new plane, which will be used for the suggested trade route flights, 'Miss Wigan', in memory of the town and its people.

*Daily Dispatch* (14 October 1932)

One of the cars made at the Westwood works between 1920 and 1926. The works were situated between the canal and the railway line at the rear of the Shepherd's Arms, Britannia Bridge.

Typical Wigan weather?

# A WEATHER NOTE

Early in 1996 a group of Wigan students went to have a look around Leicester University. At the time the country was in the grip of Arctic weather conditions. There was a severe frost, and biting winds cut one to the bone.

When they arrived at Leicester, our group bumped into a party of students from Surrey.

'What terrible, terrible weather,' said the Southerners, 'We've just driven up from Surrey. Where have you come from?'

'We've come from Wigan.'

'Oh, well, you'll be used to it,' came the laconic comment.

And finally . . .

## *Where Is Wigan?*

Well, according to an article in the *Guardian* of 25 May 1996: 'Wigan is almost at the centre of Britain, close to Pennington Flash country park. . . .'

# DO YOU KNOW? – ANSWERS

**page 18** Standish parish church is in the township of Langtree; the boundary runs through the Market Place.

**page 26** The Hall is the correct name of Wigan Rectory.

**page 42** Hell or Ell Meadow Lock is on the canal near the junction of Scot Lane and Woodhouse Lane.

**page 58** Coalmining History quiz
1. 1947
2. Bryn Hall Colliery
3. 75
4. 344
5. Types of safety lamp
6. He was short of money
7. Ludovic
8. The workings were shaped like a honeycomb and are the only known example of this type.
9. They were collieries in Hindley, Blackrod and Whelley.
10. Colliery locomotives. (At Orrell Colliery).
11. 1958
12. 1946
13. 1929
14. 1962
15. 1959
16. 1962
17. 1958
18. 1955
19. 1989
20. 1970
21. A tin in which the collier carried his food.
22. Disused underground workings.
23. A basket or small wooden wagon for moving coal about the pit.
24. Unriddled coal containing slack.
25. A man responsible for loading and unloading coal at the surface.
26. Hessian material impregnated with tar and used to make partitions to aid ventilation.
27. Lumpy coal.
28. A small geological fault
29. A workman paid by the day
30. A seam of coal appearing on the surface.

**page 67.** May Mill, Pemberton, Rylands, Gidlow Mill, and Dicconson Mills, Aspull.

**page 74.**
1. The authentic ones are Hallgate, Stairgate, Millgate and Wallgate.
2. Highgate is Manchester Road, Higher Ince, and Watergate is Chorley Lane, Worthington.
3. 'Wiend' means an alley.

4. Robbing Lane is Ormskirk Road, Pemberton.
5. Fairbrother Lane.
6. A path that joined Gidlow Lane with Wigan Lane opposite the junction with Leyland Mill Lane.
7. Bolton Road, Aspull.
8. Cabbage Lane roughly followed the route of Wrightington Street.

**page 96.** Norman Green, who hid himself under the floorboards of his house in Higher Ince for eight years in the mistaken belief that the police suspected him of a serious crime.

**page 102.** Oysters.

**page 108.**
1. Professional musicians paid by the Wigan Corporation to entertain the inhabitants (in the seventeenth and eighteenth centuries).
2. The bellman (i.e. town crier).
3. They were law-enforcement officers. The word is a corruption of by-law men.

**page 139.** Town Centre Pubs
1. Grand Hotel
2. All Saint's Tavern
3. Bricklayers' Arms
4. Crofters' Arms
5. White Lion
6. Black Horse
7. Dog and Partridge
8. Clarence Hotel
9. Victoria Hotel
10. Swan and Railway
11. Wheatsheaf
12. Shakespeare
13. Brewers' Arms
14. Derby Arms
15. Horseshoe
16. Bath Hotel
17. Ship Hotel
18. White Horse
19. Market Hotel
20. Park Hotel
21. Three Crowns
22. Legs of Man (Top and Bottom!)
23. Commercial Hotel
24. Fleece Hotel
25. Ring o' Bells
26. Old Dog
27. Cross Keys
28. Raven
29. Golden Lion
30. Minorca

**page 146.** Roller hockey (i.e. hockey in which the players wore roller skates).

**page 154.** George Orwell in *The Road to Wigan Pier* (on page 75).

# SOURCES

Anderson, Donald, *Coal* (Newton Abbot, 1982)

Anderson, Donald, *The Orrell Coalfield, Lancashire, 1740–1850* (Buxton, 1975)

Anderson, Donald, J. Lane and A.A. France, *The Standish Collieries, Wigan, Lancashire 1635–1963) (*Ashton-in-Makerfield, 1984*)*

Arrowsmith, Josiah (Ed.), *Register of the Parish Church of Wigan,* Lancashire Parish Register Society Publications: 4 (1899)

Bagley, J.J., *A History of Lancashire* (London, 1956)

Blakeman, R., *St Mary's Church, Ince Centenary 1887–1987* (Ince-in-Makerfield, 1987)

Bridgeman, George T.O., *History of the Church and Manor of Wigan . . .* , Chetham Society Publications N.S. 15, 16, 17 and 18 (1888–1890)

Brierley, Alice (Ed.), *Register of the Church of St Thomas the Martyr, Upholland, 1600–1735,* Publications of the Lancashire Parish Register Society, 25 (1905)

Brierley, Henry, *Registers of the Parish Church of Standish 1560–1653*, Lancashire Parish Register Society Publications, 46 (1912)

Challinor, Raymond, *The Lancashire and Cheshire Miners* (Newcastle-upon-Tyne, 1972)

Charity Commission, *Endowed Charities, Returns* (London, 1908)

Children's Employment Commission, *Appendix to the First Report of the Commissioners. Mines. Part II. Reports and Evidence from Sub-Commissioners* (London, 1842)

Clark, George Thomas, *Report to the General Board of Health on a preliminary inquiry into the sewage, drainage and supply of water, and the sanitary condition of the inhabitants of the Borough of Wigan* (London, 1849)

Clarke, Mike, *The Leeds and Liverpool Canal* (Preston, 1990)

Derbyshire, George, *Wigan in Military History* (5 vols, unpub, 1949–74)

*Diary of Roger Lowe of Ashton-in-Makerfield, Lancashire, 1663–78* (Ashton-in-Makerfield, 1994)

Dodd, William, *The Factory System . . .* (London, 1842)

Farrer, William (Ed.), *The Cartulary of Cockersand Abbey. . .* , Chetham Society Publications 38, 39, 40, 43, 56, 57 and 64 (1898–1909)

Fitzhugh, Terrick V.H., *Dictionary of Genealogy* (London, 1991)

Farrer, William and J. Brownbill, *Victoria History of the County of Lancashire* (8 vols, London, 1906–14)

Fishwick, Henry, *Pleadings and Depositions in the Duchy Court of Lancaster time of Henry VII and Henry VIII,* Rec. Soc. Lancs. and Ches. 32 (1896)

Friar, Stephen, *The Batsford Companion to Local History* (London, 1991)

Hawkes, Arthur J., 'Medieval history of Pemberton', *Wigan Examiner* (July and August 1951)

Hayes, Wilson J., *Winstanley the Digger* (London, 1979)

Hornsey, B., 'A Brief History of the Cinemas of Wigan', *Mercia Bioscope 54* pp. 1–9 (Feb. 1995)

Hunter, Derek, *Politics and the Working Class in Wigan 1890–1914* (Unpub. MA dissertation, 1974.)

Jones, G.C. and J. Price, 'Excavations at the Wiend, Wigan 1982–4', *Greater Manchester Archaeological Journal 1* (1985)

Kenyon, Denise, *The Origins of Lancashire* (Manchester, 1991)

Langton, William (Ed.) *The Visitation of Lancashire . . . AD 1533 . . .* Chetham Society Publications 98 (1876)

Orwell, George, *The Road to Wigan Pier* (London, 1937)

*Pictorial History of the County of Lancaster* (London, 1844)

*Polite Society by Arthur Devis, 1712–1787*, Catalogue of the exhibition, Harris Museum and Art Gallery, Preston, Lancs. (1983)

Porteus, T.C., 'The Mysterious murder of Sir William de Bradshaigh', *Trans. Lancs. and Ches. Ant. Soc. 56* pp. 1–24 (1944)

Porteus, T.C., *Traveller's tales of Wigan* (Wigan, 1925)

Price, William, 'Some notes on the places, traditions and folklore of the Douglas Valley', *Trans. Lancs. and Ches. Hist. Soc. N.S. 15* (1901)

Prince, John Critchley, *The Poetical Works of John Critchley Prince*, 2 vols (Manchester, 1880)

Saul, Pauline and F.C. Markwell, *The Family Historian's Enquire Within* (Newbury, 1991)

Sparke, Archibald (Ed.), *Registers of the Parish Church of Deane*, Lancashire Parish Register Society Publications, 54 (1917)

Stretch, E.K., *The Tramways of Wigan* (Rochdale, 1979)

Townley, C.H.A., F.D. Smith and J.A. Peden, *The Industrial Railways of the Wigan Coalfield* (2 vols, Cheltenham, 1991 and 1992)

Tupling, G.H. 'Lancashire Markets in the 16th and 17th centuries', *Trans. Lancs. and Ches. Ant. Soc., 58 and 59* (1947)

Tupling, G.H. *South Lancashire in the Reign of Edward II*, Chetham Society Publications 1 (1949)

Walker, J.S.F. and A.S. Tindall (Eds.) *Country Houses of Greater Manchester* (Manchester, 1985)

Watkin, W. Thompson, *Roman Lancashire* (Liverpool, 1883)

Webb, Yvonne and Dawn Whitwham, *Wigan at War* (Wigan, 1994)

Weeton, Ellen, *Miss Weeton: Journal of a Governess*, 2 vols. (Oxford, 1936)

Worall, E.S. (Ed.), *Returns of Papists 1767 Diocese of Chester*, Catholic Record Society Publications Occ. Pub. 1 (1980)